To The Next Village

21st Century Church Planting Missions

Steven Mills

To The Next Village

21st Century Church Planning Missions

Steven Mills

Copyright © 2020 by Steven Mills

ISBN: 9781615292288

Vision Publishing
P.O. Box 1680
Ramona, CA 92065
1 760 789-4700
www.booksbyvision.org

Table of Contents

Introduction

Why a book on Church Planting Strategies for the 21st Century?

Each day 175,000 people die without Jesus. If each of these people was put in a body bag and the body bags were laid side by side, they would form a line stretching for 40 miles. New church planting strategies are needed to reach these people. The most effective way to reach the unreached peoples of the world is through church planting.

Strategies provide an overall blueprint. Strategies not only make clear what needs to be done; they help evaluate how well it was accomplished. Strategy normally comes in one of two ways: 1) Mission agency staff research, prayer, and planning; 2) Field workers growing in practical knowledge, and concrete experience.

This work is undertaken after nearly twenty years of full-time missionary work in Africa. During those years, many things were learned from those who went before, and many things were learned by trial and error. This work will draw upon years of personal experience and the research from many different mission organizations.

Who Moved My Missions?

Over the past two or three decades there has been a dramatic shift in the way World Missions is done. In 2003 on a plane to Kuwait with another missionary, David Pursifull to hold a cell conference in Kuwait City, there was a discussion about the changes that have taken place in missions during the last 20 years. During this discussion the book, "Who Moved My Cheese?" and how it deals with change in the workplace was talked about. David made the comment, "I feel like someone has moved my mission." He went on to suggest a book called "Who Moved My Mission?" be written to investigate the changing paradigms of missions. Since then he has written an article in the Global 12 Project magazine titled "Who Moved My Mission?" The beginning of this work was a result of that discussion.

You Can't Ride A Donkey in A Star Wars World!

Veteran Missionary Rev. Ron Bishop preached a wonderful message about paradigm shifts and the changing tide in missions at the Destiny Church Annual Missions Conference, San Antonio in 2003. The title of his message was "You Can't Ride a Donkey in a Star Wars World!" The premise of the message dealt with moving on with the times in which we live and minister to be relevant to our current situation. We can no longer rely on doing things as usual if we want to effectively reach the utter most parts of the earth with the Gospel of Jesus Christ.

Ron showed a series of pictures of different donkeys showing how we sometimes try to use old methods to reach modern societies. As you look at these pictures you will want to laugh at the picture, but they make you stop to think about your own life and ministry. Take a moment to look over these pictures and captions. Allow the Holy Spirit to speak to your heart and spirit about things in your life and ministry that need to change so you can be more effective for God.

Old fashioned methods won't carry today's load. Many times, we become over-whelmed with the work when we try to use the methods of the past to do the tasks of today. God will always give us today's method to carry today's load. If we continue to pile things on to an already overloaded paradigm, we are in danger of losing control of the situation.

Sometimes we are guilty of trying to pull our old methods into our new responsibilities. Human nature has a way of trying to always use the things we are used to using even when we know they will not do a good job. If you must strain and fuss to get your strategy to work in your new area of ministry, maybe it is time to look for something new.

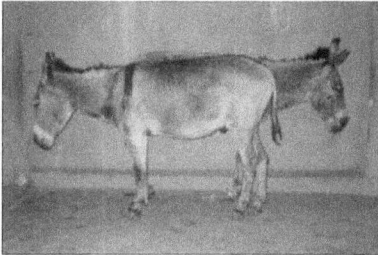

Which way do I go? With all the changes taking place in the world and in missions some people feel like they have lost their way. Missionaries and church planters can feel pulled in every direction. There are so many needs and so few workers the tendency is to try to do everything. There is a danger of being a "Jack of all trades" but a master of none.

Does your donkey need to be turned out to pasture? Sometimes we just need to turn the old methods out to pasture. From time to time we need to upgrade to a new model. Do not use the excuse, "We never did that before." Be willing to let go of the old and embrace the new. Our message, the Gospel, never changes but our methods must fit our current situation.

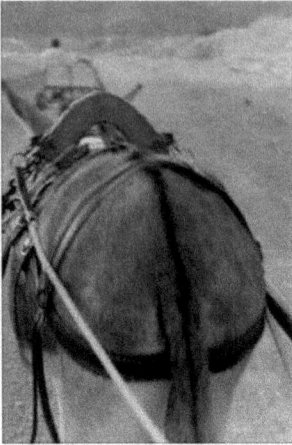

Tired of this view? Try something new! It has been said that one of the characteristics of insanity is doing the same thing over and over expecting different results each time. If that definition were applied to missions, there would be many mission organizations that would be certified insane. When we continue to do the same things and use the same methods year after year, we can only expect the same results. For new results we need to be bold enough to step outside the box trying new ideas. God works best outside the box!

There are veteran missionaries on the field who are still holding to the old paradigms of Church Planting Strategies. At the same time, there are fresh recruits who are going out with a new understanding of missions. Both groups feel that their way is best and often the two are never able to work together. This book is intended to examine both paradigms, evaluate the good and bad in both, and come up with what the author feels is the proper balance for 21st Century Missions.

We Live in An Ever Changing World

One thing I have learned for sure – nothing stays the same. My university biology professor once made the statement that everything in the universe that is alive is in a constant state of change. There is only one exception to that statement, the Word of God never changes yet is alive and powerful. With that understanding the underlying Biblical principles of this work will never change even if the methods or means of communicating those principles change.

The world is ever changing, if you do not believe it just look at a map from 25 years ago. There are many new names for nations, some new nations, new borders, and some old nations have been divided into several smaller nations. The fall of communism in the Soviet Block, independence in Africa, a market economy in China and the rise of the Euro are just some of the drastic changes in our world. The church needs to be on the cutting edge of what God is doing and be willing to change the way we do things to be relevant to our ever-changing world.

Are We Stuck in A Rut?

Sometimes the church is stuck in its ways of doing missions and is not willing to change. A couple of years ago I was attending a Pastors Conference when one of the leaders made this statement, "The doorknob is still on the outside of my church and if people want to get saved they can come in." I was shocked and appalled. With thinking like that in the pulpit there is no wonder we have so much trouble getting people to go out and win souls. The same type of attitude is shown by many missionaries and mission organizations when they are still doing missions the same way after 50 to 100 years. They have a feeling that the new mission ideas are trying to make them obsolete and unneeded.

On the other hand, the new people going out are missing out on much wisdom and understanding when they do not listen to the older generation of missionaries. We can learn from the past victories and failures to be better prepared to implement the strategies God is showing us in the 21st Century. The bottom line is that we need the entire body of Christ to be effective in this end time harvest of billions of souls.

Chapter 1
God's Vision for The World

Vision – What Does God Want to Do?

> *"And I tell you that you are Peter and on this rock I will build my church, and the gates of Hades will not overcome it".* (Matthew 16:18)

> *"But You will receive power when the Holy Spirit comes upon you; and you will be my witnesses in Jerusalem, and in all Judea and Samaria, and to the ends of the earth".* (Acts 1:8)

> *"All authority under heaven and on earth has been given to me. Therefore go and make disciples of all nations, baptizing them in the name of the Father and of the Son and of the Holy Spirit, and teaching them to obey everything I have commanded you. And surely I will be with you always, to the very end of the age". Jesus* (Mathew 28:18-20)

God's Vision for the World

We live in an exciting time in the world. Even in the midst of much upheaval (or perhaps because of it), God is moving powerfully across the globe. Certainly, we all sense the quickening of God's move and anticipate the culmination of the commission given by Jesus and His eventual return. We are actively pursuing to fulfill our role by desiring to plant vibrant churches that will usher many lives into the kingdom of God throughout the world. That is the reason we are here. But as we begin, let us be sure to set our focus on this question: "What does God want to do?"

"Catching a vision" is all about understanding what God wants to do. True vision comes from God. He reveals what He wants to do for a particular group of people. Then we accept His assignment to participate with Him in seeing His will done.

Why Plant New Churches?

As we can see from the introductory verses above, Jesus is determined to build His church throughout the world. And how is He going to do that? Scripture clearly says by sending us, even to the ends of the earth, to be His witnesses and to make disciples. The Commission is great, but we have a great God! But why should our focus be on establishing new local churches? One obvious answer to this question is that new churches need to be planted in areas where a self-sustaining, gospel teaching church does not yet exist. Such areas are certainly the highest priority. Every local church should be committed to planting churches in unreached and neglected areas of the world.

But consider also some other facts related to planting new churches. One denomination found that 80% of its converts came to faith in Jesus in churches less than two years old. The simple fact is that all measures show that planting a new church is the best method of evangelism! Church planting is all about reaching people with the life-changing power of the gospel of Christ. It is not about reaching our annual quota of churches. Our focus is people, and planting churches provides a much better harvest than existing churches simply growing larger. In fact, established congregations can grow fastest by multiplying themselves rather than remaining as a single larger congregation. It is a matter of multiplication versus addition. Further, new churches often speak to the next generation of young people as well as different ethnic or economic groups better than older churches. These factors, plus many others, point toward church-planting as the best way to send forth workers into the ripened fields and bring in the harvest!

Keeping It Simple

Jesus declared that His purpose in ministry was to seek and save those who were spiritually lost (Luke 19:10). He also stated that

He would build His church on the earth (Matthew 16:18). Let that verse in Matthew remind us that His role in church planting is greater than ours. Jesus is sending us out in the same way the Father sent Him; we are to simply do the works of Jesus. Jesus calls us in Acts 1:8 to be His witnesses and in Matthew 28:19 to make disciples of all nations. It really is that simple. We often tend to overcomplicate Christ's straightforward call to the church. Having said that, there are clearly many details involved with planting and developing a church. Let us begin this church planting seminar by setting these two basic objectives in the forefront of our thinking: to be His witness and to make disciples of all nations (ethnos). These are God's will and purposes for us, and He has enabled us to fulfill them.

God's Vision for Our World

Have you ever considered what God's vision for your nation may be? A vision is a picture of the future that God has put in your heart. What do you "see" when you think about the future of the body of Christ in your nation? Is it a victorious church being sent by the Holy Spirit with the gospel throughout the nation and world?

Blessed to be a Blessing

God sees a church that is the head, not the tail. A church that is a "sender," not just a "receiver." It is evident that God has been doing a great work in the world over the past 25 years. He has raised up a strong and vibrant church and is pouring out a blessing upon the nations. But why? Like God's covenant with Abraham, He blesses His people in order that they can be a blessing to others. We are blessed to be a blessing.

We believe that God's vision is to win the world – all of it! That means that the church must be mobilized to reach the neglected, even "undesirable," communities that are spread throughout primarily the interior of every nation. But there is more. We believe that the church of every nation will be a mighty force in this move of God throughout the earth that will usher in the return of Christ. Will we rise to the task set before us? Will we heed the commission of Christ? As we are faithful with what the Lord has put before us today, He will raise us up for even greater work tomorrow.

Your Church is on a Mission

> *"As you sent me into the world, I have sent them into the world"*. (John 17:18)

The call is clear. It is from the very mouth of Jesus. He has sent us into the world just as the Father sent Him. That is the mission for each of us as well as for your church. God wants you and your church to be advancing the kingdom in your community and beyond. But it is not a task that can be completed by a single church. God desires the body of Christ to partner together to complete the commission. That is the only way we can fulfill the call.

The church was created to be a vehicle to fulfill this call. Its vision is to inspire and facilitate a movement of churches that raise leaders to plant churches that raise leaders to plant churches. We invite you to join us as we follow the call of the Lord Jesus to go and make disciples throughout every nation and even to the ends of the earth!

Values – Why Are We Committed to this Mission?

What Values Are and Are Not

Values are different than vision and mission. Mission deals with what you want to do. Values answer the question, "Why do I want to do that?" Values are the "why" behind the "what." Consider values in this way. At the end of your life, what did you really stand for? These are your values. Or in a more practical manner, review a typical week or month in your schedule. What you spent the most time, money, and effort on are your core values.

Values are consistent, passionate, Biblical, and distinctive convictions that:

- determine our priorities

- influence our decisions

- drive our ministry

- are always demonstrated in our behavior

Values are not:

- your statement of faith, doctrine, or theology. What is "believed" is not necessarily a value. A belief becomes a value when it is truly acted upon.

- your vision, purpose, or missions' statement. Values are the attitudes behind the actions.

- methods or programs through which you minister. The methods and programs are only the delivery systems of your values.

The Values of Church Planting Movements

We would like to take this opportunity to share with you the value statements every church planting movement should have. Each statement contains the resultant action and a description of the heart behind each value.

Because we value authentic relationships, we will seek to create environments that foster humility, encouragement, accountability, unity and friendship for pastors and leaders (John 15:15-17; Luke 22:24-27).

Relationships are a fundamental core value of the church. We desire to carry this same value into church planting. In John 15, Jesus gave the command to His disciples – love one another. That was to be their priority in their relationships with one another. We seek to follow this command as well. The desired result will be relationships built upon humility, encouragement, and unity.

Luke 22 records a dispute that broke out among the disciples during the Last Supper as to which of them was considered the greatest. How these words still echo true too often today! Once again, Jesus set the example and brought needed correction when He clearly declared, "You are not to be like that. I am among you as one who serves." We value servant leadership. We believe that the leadership style of Jesus was to lead, not push. Accordingly, it is our desire to inspire, facilitate and organize a movement of churches that will heed the words of Jesus and reach the unreached.

Because we value equipping and releasing leaders, we will provide various training opportunities for pastors and church planters that are designed to release laborers for the harvest (Matthew 9:35-38; 2 Timothy 2:2).

Multiplication of leadership is another fundamental value in the church that we embrace. Few Bible passages share more of the heart of church planting than Matthew 9:35-38. Jesus was teaching, preaching, and healing in towns and villages when He saw the multitudes of lost people. Matthew describes the people as afflicted and helpless, like sheep without a shepherd. What was Jesus' solution? First, He had already been training and pouring Himself into them. Second, He brought awareness to the disciples of the harvest and the need to pray for laborers. Then, He sent them out to minister as an answer to the prayer! Truly, the reason Jesus called the disciples to Him, was to send them out from Him. We need to be prepared, understand the needs, pray for the laborers, and then do our part to reach the afflicted and helpless.

A model for training that we support is found in 2 Timothy 2:2. The Apostle Paul exhorts Timothy to pass on what he has learned from Paul to other faithful leaders who are able to pass them on to others. Four generations of leadership are represented in this verse. It is the desire of Church planting movements to "pass on" all the resources and mentoring possible to faithful leaders who are committed to investing themselves into other leaders for the glory of God.

Because we value all people, we will commit our resources to take the gospel and to establish life-giving, vibrant churches to peoples of unreached and neglected areas (John 4; Acts 1:8).

Reaching all people, including the lost and neglected, is a core value of church planting. One of the best examples of this in the life of Jesus is found in John 4 when He met the Samaritan women at the well. It is hard for us to understand how gross of a cultural norm Jesus broke when He asked her for a drink (v.9). Jews were not to associate with Samaritans even though Samaria was near Judea and Galilee. Jesus risked the accusations of others, even the disciples, to reach this woman and her village (He stayed for two days and many believed in Him). He willingly went to the rejected and despised people of the region. Please notice His rebuke to the disciples; "Do not say, 'Four months more and then the harvest'? I tell you, open your eyes and look at the fields! They are ripe for harvest." We need to open our eyes.

With this in mind, reconsider Jesus' commission to the disciples in Acts 1:8. They were commissioned to be His witnesses "in Jerusalem, and in all of Judea and Samaria, and to the ends of the earth." It is typically taught that Jesus was commanding them to take the gospel to successively farther distances from Jerusalem – first Judea, then Samaria, then to the ends of the earth. But an understanding of geography and a grammatical review of the passage lead to a more accurate conclusion. First, Samaria was between Judea and Galilee – it was not remote by any means. Anyone traveling to Jerusalem from the north had to go through Samaria. In fact, geographically it was in the same region as Judea. It was, however, despised by the Jews. Second, grammatically Judea and Samaria are linked in verse 8. Jesus even emphasized "all" of Judea and Samaria. These factors lead to the conclusion that Jesus was only specifying three areas – not four – in Acts 1:8.

Jesus was, in essence, saying, "Be my witnesses first right here where you are, then in this region, even the undesirable and neglected areas of your region, then to the ends of the earth."

Network - The Power of Partnership

A Dream to Reach the World

Today there are still over 4,000,000,000 people in the world who have limited or no access to the gospel. Church planting is an effective tool to achieve the goal of reaching every Unreached People Group of the world.

Why Should We Be in Partnership?

There is a new paradigm of missions that is taking hold! It is a vibrant, strategic model that goes right to the heart of the harvest: PEOPLES! This model has emerged from the very heart of God for all peoples. In the world's 234 geopolitical nations, there exist over 17,000 distinct, ethnic cultures.

These are the people groups The Great Commission is directed towards on earth. "Go therefore and make disciples of all the nations (ethnic or people groups), baptizing them in the name of the Father and the Son and the Holy Spirit" (Matthew 28:19 NAS).

These are the people groups The Great Completion will gather together in heaven." After this I beheld, and lo, a great multitude, which no man could number, of all nations, and kindreds, and people, and tongues, stood before the throne. . ." (Revelation 7:9a KJV).

The goal is to see multitudes of church planters trained and churches planted throughout the world, especially among the unreached and neglected peoples, until there are no more churches that need to be planted.

What if you could meet with other churches and church planters who share your passion for a particular people group? What if you could hear their stories, pray together, share resources for mobilization, and learn from their experience? What if you could find out how the skill and experience you bring to the field can best be utilized into a long-term strategic effort to reach the people group you have adopted? What if you could receive training to plant new churches to reach these unreached peoples? What if you could work closely with a team of men who share your same passion and vision with a leader who will train you and help you to plant churches? This is why we need to partner together. It is the power of partnership.

The Situation on Earth in the Year 2000[i]

The World Population in the year 2000 was 6.055 billion. The population of the world is broken into four groups.

1. There are approximately six hundred million committed Christians in the world today. They make up about ten percent of the world's population. These are the people God wants to use to take the gospel to the ends of the earth.

2. There are approximately one point two billion nominal Christians in the world today. These are people who say they are Christians, but they are not true followers who are living for Jesus. These people can be reached through neighborhood evangelism.

3. There are two point two billion non-Christians in the world today. These are people who are not Christians, but they have access to the gospel, but they have not accepted Jesus Christ as savior. These people can be reached through neighborhood evangelism.

4. There are two billion unreached people in the world today. These are people who are members of people groups who have not been penetrated by the gospel in a meaningful way. These people can be reached through cross-cultural ministers who come from group one.

Groups one, two and three, make up sixty seven percent of the of the world's population. They are considered reached with the gospel. Ninety percent of all Christian workers are ministering among these people groups.

Group four represents thirty three percent of the world's population. They are considered unreached with the gospel. Only ten percent of Christian workers are ministering among these groups.

If you are one of the many missionaries or mission executives who sometimes feel like throwing up your hands, shouting "Who Moved My Mission?" or you feel as if you are still riding a donkey in a Star Wars world come along with me on a journey of discovery. Together we can discover what God is giving as Church Planting Strategies for the 21st Century.

Money and Missions[ii]

What Christians Earn – Annual Income of all Church Members: $42 trillion.[iii]

What Christians Give - Given to any Christian causes: $700 billion.[iv]

NOTE: Americans have recently spent more money buying Halloween costumes for their pets than the amount given to reach the unreached. That is also how much we spend in America on Christmas each year.

What Christians Give to Missions –$45 billion – That's only 6.4% of the money given to Christian causes of any kind (2015).[v] *5.6% reported in 2010, GAC[vi]

NOTE: That's also how much we spend in America on dieting programs. This is also the amount of money embezzled by church workers each year.[vii]

How Christian Giving is Used[viii]

- Pastoral ministries of local churches (mostly in Christian nations): $677 billion (96.8%)

- "Home Missions" in same Christian nations: $20.3 billion (2.9%)

- Going to Unevangelized Non-Christian world: $2.1 billion (.3%)

This is different than "Unreached"

- Money that goes toward Unreached Peoples: Estimated $450 million[ix]

- In 2001 only 1% of giving to "Missions" went to unreached - if that trend holds true today it would be $450 million.

- The estimated $450 million going toward UPG's is only .001% of the $42 trillion Income of Christians.

- For every $100,000 that Christians make, they give $1 to the unreached.

Hypothetical Observations

Evangelical Christians could provide all the funds needed to plant a church in each of the 6,900 unreached people groups with only 0.03% of their income.

The Church has roughly 3,000 times the financial resources and 9,000 times the manpower needed to finish the Great Commission.

If every evangelical gave 10% of their income to missions, we could easily support 2 million new missionaries.

Chapter 2
Prayer Is the Foundation

There are many books about prayer so I will not spend much time on the subject. However, prayer needs to be mentioned because without the proper foundation no building can stand. Every church planting effort must be started, implemented, and maintained in prayer.

The first step in any church planting strategy is to recruit a prayer army. This should be done before training church planters or raising financial support for the church planting movement. The most powerful thing any one can do for unreached people groups with no gospel witness is pray. Jesus commanded us to pray to the Lord of the harvest to send forth workers into the harvest fields of the world. We do not need to pray for the harvest which is already ripe and waiting to be picked. The need is for workers who will forsake all to see the harvest brought in.

Intercessors understand that when they pray, they place themselves between God and the unreached people group. Prayer warriors stand in the gap offering protection and hope for the people group. The battle must be won in prayer before the first church planter begins to work with a people group. The old saying, "The battle is won on our knees", is especially true when talking about church planting in unreached people groups and in areas hostile to the Gospel.

There are ten thousand unreached people groups that are desperate for the gospel. We need an army of prayer warriors who will pray to the lord of the harvest to send forth workers. These prayer warriors need to take authority over the principalities and powers of darkness that have these people groups in bondage.

Stand up as a child of God commanding the people of the earth to worship the living God. The following scriptures give us license to command the peoples of the earth to worship the living God. (Note: these quotations are from The New King James Bible[x])

Psalm 96:7-10 – Give to the LORD, O families of the peoples, Give to the LORD glory and strength. Give to the LORD the glory *due* His name; Bring an offering, and come into His courts. Oh, worship the LORD in the beauty of holiness! Tremble before Him, all the earth. Say among the nations, "The LORD reigns; The world also is firmly established, It shall not be moved; He shall judge the peoples righteously."

Psalm 98:4-6 –Shout joyfully to the LORD, all the earth; Break forth in song, rejoice, and sing praises. Sing to the LORD with the harp, With the harp and the sound of a psalm, With trumpets and the sound of a horn; Shout joyfully before the LORD, the King.

Psalm 100:1-5 –Make a joyful shout to the LORD, all you lands! Serve the LORD with gladness; Come before His presence with singing. Know that the LORD, He *is* God; *It is* He *who* has made us, and not we ourselves; *We are* His people and the sheep of His pasture. Enter into His gates with thanksgiving, *And* into His courts with praise. Be thankful to Him, *and* bless His name. For the LORD *is* good; His mercy *is* everlasting, And His truth *endures* to all generations.

Ps 117:1-2 –Praise the LORD, all you Gentiles! Laud Him, all you peoples! For His merciful kindness is great toward us, And the truth of the LORD *endures* forever. Praise the LORD!

Matthew 6:5-6 – "And when you pray, you shall not be like the hypocrites. For they love to pray standing in the synagogues and on the corners of the streets, that they may be seen by men. Assuredly, I say to you, they have their reward. But you, when you pray, go into your room, and when you have shut your door, pray to your Father who *is* in the secret *place;* and your Father who sees in secret will reward you openly.

Matthew 6:31-33 - "Therefore do not worry, saying, 'What shall we eat?' or 'What shall we drink?' or 'What shall we wear?' "For after all these things the Gentiles seek. For your heavenly Father knows that you need all these things. "But seek first the kingdom of God and His righteousness, and all these things shall be added to you. "Therefore do not worry about tomorrow, for tomorrow will worry about its own things. Sufficient for the day is its own trouble.

Remember, prayer is the first step in any strategy for church planting, but it is not the entire strategy. For our prayer to be truly effective we must be willing to put feet to our prayer. During my four years in Bible College I was a member of a prayer group for Africa. Each Tuesday night we would ask God to send forth workers into the harvest fields of Africa. In my Senior year I accepted the call of God to be one of those workers I had been praying for. I had never asked God to send me to Africa, I simply asked Him to send workers. God sent me, one of His workers, to Africa to be an answer to my own prayer. We need to be careful what we pray for as sometimes God will use us to answer our own prayer. Are you willing?

Many times, as a missionary I share about the work we are involved with. People all the time tell me they would like to support us but do not have the money so all they can do is pray for us. I am quick to tell them that prayer is the greatest support they can give to a missionary. Without prayer support the missionary is helpless.

Prayer is the foundation upon which a successful church planting strategy is built.

Consecrate yourself to God in solitary prayer and fasting. Every ministry that rocked the world was preceded with solitary prayer and fasting: John in the deserts of Jordan, Jesus in the wilderness of Judea, Paul in the deserts of Arabia. Prayer and fasting cleanse the will, discipline the body and spirit, and rearrange priorities.[xi]

What we pray about reveals our priorities (such as health, money, family, good weather). Our prayer should be informed, persistent and expectant.[xii]

Chapter 3
Effective Communication of the Gospel

The overall purpose of having a strategy is to better communicate the Gospel to a lost and dying world. When Jesus left this earth, he gave us the Great Commission. For the Great Commission to be fulfilled we must communicate the Gospel to the world.

Many people argue that we do not need to waste our time and efforts with plans and strategies for church planting. They say God has called us to preach the gospel and that is all we need to know. This type of person thinks, "As long as you preach the gospel everywhere you go you will be effective in reaching the world and planting churches." Some church leaders seem to think that talking about strategies for church planting implies the use of worldly marketing techniques and gimmicks. You can hear them say, "All we need is the Holy Spirit. We must walk in the Spirit not by sight or by man's understanding. Just preach the Gospel; God will take care of the rest."

It is true that God has called up to preach the Gospel. The problem comes with our understanding of what the word preach means. We cannot fulfill the Great Commission simply by preaching. There must be effective communication before people will understand the Gospel and turn their life over to Jesus. The following statement explains this concept in a tremendous way.

The Word Preach does not just mean 'one-way verbal communication' – as in a sermon or evangelistic address. It has a much broader sense – 'to effectively communicate'. If the receivers have not understood the message, real communication has probably not occurred. The word 'communicate' also has a root meaning that helps us; that of 'communing' or interacting over 'common' ground.[xiii]

Throughout the Bible we see illustrations of this truth. The Old Testament Prophets used many different types of illustrations and object lessons. Jesus taught using parables and things the people understood. The Apostle Paul used links in the culture to proclaim the gospel. An example was on Mars Hill when he brought their attention to the statue of the unknown God. He then proceeded to introduce them to this unknown god named Jesus Christ.

We only need to study the scripture and church history to see that God uses many different strategies to communicate with different people. The communication strategy that worked for the Jews was different from the communication strategy for the gentiles. Sometimes Jesus visited the synagogue and sometimes he visited the marketplace. His message in each place was the same but the method (strategy) for communicating the message was tailor made for the audience.

There is a need to make sure we do not substitute strategies and methods for the direction and inspiration of the Holy Spirit. They are not a substitute but when used under the leading for the Holy Spirit they make us more effective in our communication of the Gospel. Over the years Missiologists have learned the importance of research and classifying people into different groups. By studying and researching these different groups the Holy Spirit can direct missionaries to the proper strategy for each group.

Always remember that there is only one Gospel – the death, burial, and resurrection of Jesus Christ. This Gospel is the power of God unto Salvation. The Gospel touches every person at their point of need. To the intellectual the Gospel can be understood and is intellectually stimulating. On the other hand, the Gospel can be comprehended by a person with diminished mental capacity. Even though this one Gospel meets the needs of every person our presentation of this Gospel should not be one size fits all.

Wilbur Schramm, one of the pioneer communicators, taught that people are only able to effectively communicate with each other when there is an area of common interest. Since we are the ones who are trying to communicate the Gospel it is up to us to make the first move to look for the area of common interest.[xiv]

This is a truly Biblical concept as seen in 1 Corinthian 9:19-23:

> *For though I am free from all, yet I have made myself servant to all, so that I might gain the more. And to the Jews I became as a Jew, so that I might gain the Jews. To those who are under the Law, I became as under the Law, so that I might gain those who are under the Law. To those who are outside Law, I became as outside Law (not being outside law to God, but under the Law to Christ), so that I might gain those who are outside Law. To the weak I became as the weak, so that I might gain the weak. I am made all things to all men, so that I might by all means save some. And this I do for the sake of the gospel, so that I might be partaker of it with you.*

Paul says he became all things to all men that he might reach them with the Gospel. Jesus became human so He might reach us with the love of God and His salvation. God is looking to each of us to present the Gospel to those around us in a way they can understand and relate to the message of salvation.

Communication is More Than Words

When we communicate with people, we must remember that communication is not only the words we speak but also involves the way we say it. Every church planter must strive to learn the language of the people they are trying to reach. By speaking to people in their own language you eliminate the problem of translation. During translation you will always have problems with meanings of words.

Language is perhaps the most significant element of any culture. A word in a church planter's birth language often cannot be translated perfectly into the birth language of people they are trying to reach. The following illustration shows the difficulty with the meaning of words during translation.

The ellipse to the left represents the meaning of the word in the church planter's language.

Meaning of the matching word in another language

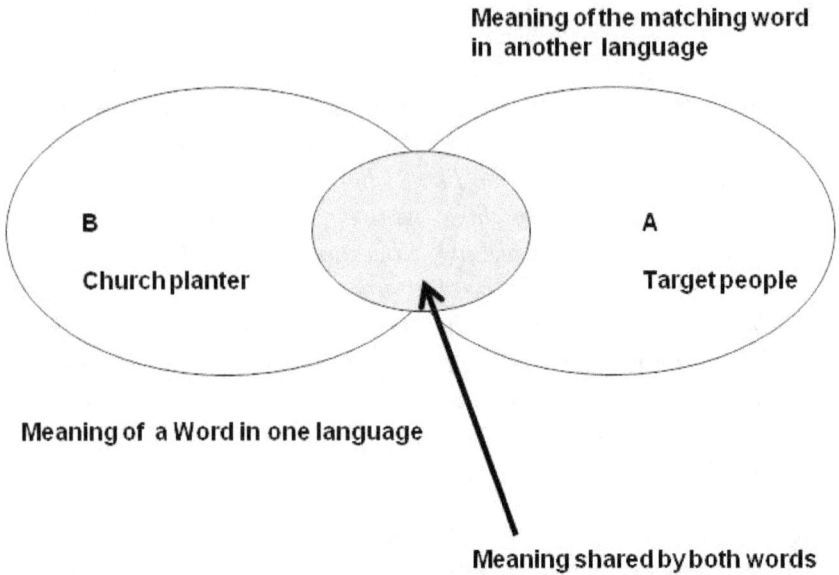

B

Church planter

A

Target people

Meaning of a Word in one language

Meaning shared by both words

- The ellipse to the right represents the closest matching word in the target people's language.

- The shaded area in the middle represents that part of the meaning of both words that is the same.

- By using their word, you add meaning to your word that you do not intend which is represented by the unshaded area B

- You also lose some meaning from your word represented by the unshaded area A[xv]

A good communicator is always mindful of and pays attention to the differences in the meaning of words. Sometimes when you communicate through a translator a word you use may take an entire sentence to translate. At other times, your entire sentence can be translated in one word. Effective communication using a translator is a skill that takes much prayer and practice. There must be a spiritual connection between the speaker, the translator, and the audience.

Another part of communication involves the way you wrap or package the message. You must make sure that you package your message is a way that is familiar to your audience. Be incredibly careful that you do not use illustrations from your culture and background that may not be familiar to them. Short term teams need to be aware of this part of communication. The things said at home may not be understood on the mission field. Some examples would be things like:

- That was an off the wall statement

- That idea was really far out

- I am out on a limb here

The people listening to you must be able to understand and comprehend the message or you are wasting your time and theirs. Watch out for colloquialisms and cultural catch phrases. You must also be careful with Christian vocabulary when ministering to an unreached people group.

We must not force upon an unreached people group our culture and worldview as we teach them the Word of God and the ways of God. This was stated nicely by Don Marchant when he said, "The people must develop a moral code and an expression of Christian beliefs that are totally scriptural, but are expressed in ways that fit their history and culture."[xvi]

Marchant goes on to say that we communicate three things when we interact with people. We communicate knowledge, we communicate feelings, and we communicate blessing or judgments. These messages are communicated not by our words but by our actions, gestures, and attitudes. Communication that is not words is called para-message. A paramessage is communication that goes along with the words we speak, and is communicated by the way we are standing or gesturing, by our tone of voice, by the words we emphasize, by the expression on our faces, even by our eyes or by our habits.

A key to effective communication of the gospel is to constantly be aware of the para messages we are sending to our hearers. Our para-messages communicate feelings and judgments such as agreement, disagreement, respect, disrespect, trust, distrust, love, hate, anger, concern, boredom.[xvii]

When the spoken message and the para-message contradict each other, three things happen:

- The receiver almost always believes the para-message, not the spoken message.

- The receiver distrusts the sender.

- The receiver remembers the para-message longer than the spoken message.[xviii]

Examples of actions that carry para-messages are: smiling, frowning, bringing a chair for someone, putting your arm around someone, pounding your fist on the table, giving someone a special gift, shaking hands with someone while looking around the room to see who else is there.[xix]

By paying close attention to our para-messages we can greatly improve the effectiveness of our communication. Ask the Holy Spirit to help you be aware of your unspoken communication. The Lord will help you change your non-verbal communication that hinders your effectiveness in communicating the Gospel story. Improvement in your communication techniques will help your ministry.

Be careful with gestures.

Make sure a gesture is acceptable in the culture before using it. Many times, in cross-cultural communication of the Gospel the message is negated because of inappropriate gestures from the speaker. Acceptable gestures in one culture are inappropriate and sometimes vulgar in another culture. The importance of research about culturally unacceptable gestures can not be overstated. It is not the responsibility of the audience to accept the gestures of the speaker but the speaker's responsibility to make sure gestures are acceptable to the audience.

Communication has two parts

The sender gives out information and the receiver needs to understand the information given. All communication passes through two different cultural filters. There is the cultural filter for the speaker and the cultural filter for the listener. Every speaker communicates according to the cultural worldview they learned growing up and the listener understands what they hear according to their cultural worldview. Therefore, all communication passes through two sets of worldview filters. Some of the meaning is filtered out by the speaker's cultural worldview and more is filtered out by the listener's cultural worldview.

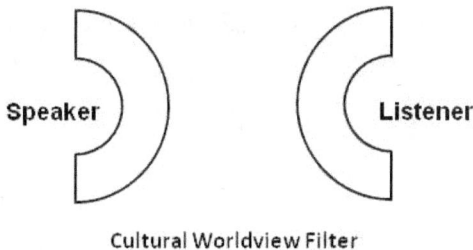

Cultural Worldview Filter

Here is one example:

The word crusade has totally different meanings to the American evangelist and North African Muslim community he wants to reach. The word crusade to the American evangelist brings up an image of a large open-air meeting where he preaches the Word of God and hundreds of people accept Jesus. The word crusade to the

North Africa Muslim brings up an image of King Richard and his crusaders invading North Africa to convert the heathen from Islam to Christianity with the edge of the sword.

As You Communicate[xx]

- Find out whether they have understood

- Take the blame for their lack of understanding

- If you seem unsuccessful at communicating, do something else.

- If you notice they are becoming hostile or uncooperative, build trust and respect

- Avoid distracting them

- Practice what you preach

- Learn from them

Statistics about communication[xxi]

WE REMEMBER	AFTER 3 HOURS	AFTER 3 DAYS
What we hear	70%	10%
What we see	72%	20%
What we see and hear	86%	65%
What we see, hear, and do	95%	85%

Within the SAME CULTURE, expect 70% of your message to be understood

Within a FOREIGN CULTURE, expect 50% or less of your message to be understood

The Communication of the Gospel Changes Culture

As you communicate the Gospel to different people groups, and they become Christians their culture will be affected by the Word of God. The Word of God lifts people from degradation to self-respect, productivity, and provision. Missiologists call this process, redemption, and lift.[xxii]

You must always remember that your FIRST PRIORITY is to share the Gospel of Jesus Christ. Make sure that you do not get caught up with meeting physical needs and lose focus on your purpose for going to a people group.

When they are saved their way of life and their culture will be redeemed and they will be lifted. God is interested in us ministering to the whole man but make sure you always minister to the whole man, spirit, soul and body.

Chapter 4
Contextualization

Contextualization in its simplest term means to communicate the Gospel in such a way that it is culturally relevant and easily understood by the audience. When the Gospel is contextualized it simply means that it is presented in language and vocabulary that is readily understood by the target audience.

In any type of communication there will be cultural barriers that must be breached. The speaker filters what he says through his culture and the hearer filters what he hears trough his culture. It is imperative that the person sharing the Gospel in a cross-cultural setting learn the culture of the person he is sharing with.

David J. Hesselgrave and Edward Rommen give a wonderful definition of culture: For the purpose of this discussion culture can be defined as the body of knowledge shared by the members of a group. That knowledge takes the form of rules which govern the way in which individuals relate to and interpret their environment. The utilization of such knowledge leads to culturally specific forms of behavior, patterns of communication (not language per se), sets of values, and types of artifacts.[xxiii]

With this idea of culture in mind we will look at a diagram showing the cultural barriers between the church planter and the target people group. It is the job of the church planter to make sure he is communicating in such a way that the target group understands the message in the context of their culture.

The tendency in the past was to change the host culture to be like the culture of the church planter. Rather than simply evangelizing people groups missionaries tended to "westernize" or "civilize" these groups in their effort to "Christianize" them. The idea was for a person to be saved they must be just like us. People were taught that their culture was bad, and the church planter's culture was "Christian". If you do not believe this look at any established mission where you will see people acting like westerners rather than like their own people. They dress like the church planter, sing the same songs (translated into their language), build the same type buildings, etc.

Missionaries need to learn to become more like the people to whom they are taking the Gospel. The church in each people group needs to be unique allowing the people to worship God in a manner that fits into their culture. Truly, there are things in every culture that need to be changed to line up with God's Word but there is also much in every culture that can be accepted and integrated into their worship.

Melvin L. Hodges said, "We believe that the gospel is universal; that the divine seed will take root and prosper in any land." The gospel seed can be adapted to every type of humanity, and to every social climate. It truly is the universal gospel seed.[xxiv]

"Evangelization is a process of bringing the gospel to people where they are, not where you would like them to be."[xxv]

"An evangelist, a missionary must respect the culture of a people, not destroy it."[xxvi]

Every people group surrounds itself with a Culture Barrier.

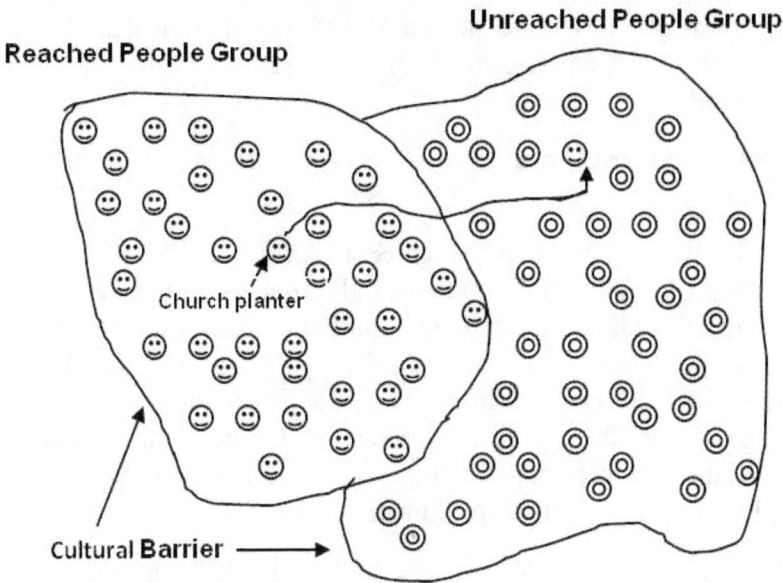

Most nations or countries have hundreds of ethnic groups. Ethnic groups know they are very separate, each one from the others, because of culture, and often because of language difference.

Missionaries learn how to overcome culture-barriers. These barriers exist in the minds or attitudes of persons who recognize that a certain individual is not a member of their own people group, but is instead a foreigner, and should therefore not be trusted. [xxvii]

Several years ago, I was paid one of the highest compliments a missionary can ever receive. During a leadership seminar in a West African country I was introduced as an African. The delegates were told that the wrapping on the outside was white but the package on the inside was African. Finally, after many years of prayer, study, and fellowship I had breached the cultural barrier and was accepted as one of their own.

The goal of contextualization of the Gospel is to plant churches that are identified with and look like the society of the people they are reaching. If we are not careful, we will transplant Western churches to the unreached people rather than planting a contextualized indigenous church.

Listen to the following testimony from a visitor to a church in China.

Before my first visit to a "Three-Self" (official) church in China, I wondered, "How will I understand what is going on without knowing the Mandarin language and the Chinese culture?" During this service, however, I was surprised to hear translated Western songs and observe worship patterned after traditional Western forms. After the service concluded, Chinese and American Christians met informally to sing familiar hymns, the Americans in English, and the Chinese in Mandarin.

What we witnessed was not a contextualized Chinese church, as we anticipated, but a replica of a transplanted, Western one. Such churches reflect the culture and heritage of the original sending church. The initial missionaries establish patterns within the target culture which mirror those of their own culture. These non-indigenous forms then become routinized as local Christians adopt them as part of the gospel. Contextualized churches, on the other hand, develop local ways for reflecting God's will by asking the very difficult question, "How does God expect His eternal will and message to be reflected in this cultural context?"

A transplanted church is like a potted plant transferred to a new culture. It is expected to grow and reproduce exactly as it did in the original culture. A contextualized church is like planting "God's seed" in new soil and allowing the seed to grow naturally, adapting to the language, thought processes, and rituals of the new culture *without losing its eternal meanings.* These eternal meanings include a biblical perspective of God, Christ, the Holy Spirit, the church, humanity, time and eternity, and salvation.

A transplanted church could also be compared to a banana plant in Canada. To survive winter, it must be taken into the house and given special care. Because it is unable to adapt to the new climate, the plant will never be able to reproduce itself. Contextualized churches, on the other hand, are like banana plants in the Bahamas. They thrive in their environment and produce much fruit.[xxviii]

The author of this article goes on to analyze four different areas where you can tell a transplanted church from a contextualized church. We must be very careful that we are patient enough to allow the local believers to take the initiative in these four areas. The four areas he lists are: Functional Arrangements, Leadership Patterns, Cognitive Approaches and Message Formulation.[xxix]

Each of these four areas will be explained briefly. These four things happen naturally unless the church planter is conscience of them and pays close attention to avoid these pitfalls.

Functional Arrangements – This is talking about the way the mission church functions. Most missionaries come into a culture and set up churches like they had back home. For example, they meet at 10 o'clock on Sunday morning and 6 o'clock on Sunday night. This is done because this is the way "church" is done back home. It would be much better to find out what fits best into the culture of the people. For example, in many Arab nations, churches meet on Friday as this is the holy day of Islam. The people already have Friday off from work for worship, so the churches meet on that day. There are churches in factory towns which have multiple services to accommodate shift workers. When pioneering a new church, we need to fit into the community rather than force the community to conform to our way of doing things.

The Holy Spirit knows what each community needs and can direct the church planter in the proper direction if he will listen. Many times, we come, or we are sent to a new culture and we arrive with a pre-conceived idea and plan of what needs to be done. How much better it would be to come to the new culture with an open mind and heart asking the Holy Spirit for direction.

Spend time in the community attending some for their community functions. Try to discover what people are interested in and what times they like to meet. We worked with one church in Kenya where one of the elders had a burden to reach the local golfers. None of them would come to church because the services were during the best time to play golf. He decided to have an early morning service for golfers to be finished in time for the best tee times. After several months, many of the golfers were attending church and the early service became the most popular service of the day.

Leadership Patterns - Here we are talking about the way the church is run. Mission churches normally have the same leadership structure of the home or sending church. This can cause problems when the sending church has a strong pastoral leadership and the church planter is going to an area that has multiple elderships as their form of government. The opposite can be true as well when the church planter comes from a church run by an elder board and goes to an area where a single chief runs the show. The church needs to reflect the leadership style of the people if it is not anti-biblical. The church needs to look as much as possible like the surrounding society while staying true to scripture.

The Bible, while giving principles of Christian leadership (Mark 10:35-45) and structure (Titus 1:5-9), was not meant to be a detailed instructional manual on leadership patterns.[xxx] The principles of scripture can not be violated while setting up the leadership structure of the new church. In the same way, we must be careful to not equate our leadership style as the only Biblical pattern.

Cognitive Approaches – Here we are talking about the way things are done. When a church planter goes into a new culture, he sees everything through his worldview. The way he was raised, the experiences he has, what he was taught in school all form the way he sees the world. When he approaches this new culture, he must be careful not to force his worldview on his audience. Church planters must be students of the culture and worldview of the society they want to reach.

The gospel must be presented in such a way as to be relevant to the society. While in Bible College one of my professors, Van Gill, told the following mission story. On one of the islands of the Pacific a church was established. The missionaries came from a very conservative background and thought it was sinful for women to wear open toed shoes. Therefore, there was a rule in their church that all women must wear closed toed shoes to service. However, there was one small problem – no one on the island wore shoes. The missionaries had to import shoes for the women so they could come to church. You would see ladies on Sunday morning walking to church with their shoes in a bag and just before entering the church they would cram their feet into these extremely uncomfortable shoes so they would be welcome in the church. In this situation, the missionaries should have adopted the worldview and culture of the local people and allowed them to come to church barefooted. To many this seems like a silly illustration but this type of thing happens all the time.

The same type of thing also happens with the music. The church planter brings songs from the sending church and culture and translates them into the local language. This can work in the beginning when the church is being established. However, the goal is for the new church to begin to write worship songs using their own language and music style. Music should be written using local instruments and rhythms. Every church should be as much like the local culture as possible while staying true to scripture.

Message Formulation - How is the message delivered? Preachers from outside normally come with messages and delivery styles from their sending church and culture. They think the only things that needs to be done is to translate the words into the new language. Often everything needs to change. Church planters must spend time studying the way the local people communicate.

When we began our ministry with the Digo in southeastern Kenya we were told these people could not be reached with the Gospel. Many groups had tried to evangelize them with no success. During our research, we discovered these groups had only used open air crusades as their method of evangelism. People would gather for the singing but as soon as the preaching would start the people would leave. We also discovered that one of the main modes of communication in the Digo society was with drama. A team was brought in to present the gospel as a drama. People started gathering during the singing and when the drama began no one left. On the second day people from other villages began to gather to see the drama. Simple research and observation revealed the way to share the gospel with these people. As a result of drama several new churches were established.

Contextualization - Making the message relate

Contextualization simply means communicating the Gospel in a way appropriate and understandable to the target audience. Contextualization is done in every area of Christian communication. Many times, the speaker is not aware they are putting the gospel into a contextualized form. Take for example the Sunday school teacher using simple language and child-related illustrations, games, and activities in her four-year-old class. A pastor contextualizes by gearing his message in such a way to meet the needs of a given audience by using certain illustrations. The presentation changes with the venue and with the audience in attendance.[xxxi]

Every time we cross cultural barriers to share the gospel, we must contextualize the gospel, so the target audience understands. Our western way of doing things is not the only way things can be accomplished. There must be consistent study of the local culture and language to be an effective witness of the gospel. It would be wise to gain the counsel of any missionaries who have worked in your area. One visiting ministry can destroy years of foundation work by not understanding the culture and not seeking guidance from resident missionaries. While working in a Muslim area in East Africa we experienced this firsthand. After spending nearly a year building relationships and bridges with the Muslim community in which we lived much of the work was destroyed in a single meeting by an International evangelist from Ireland. Somehow, he received permission to hold the first large open-air crusade in the area. During his first meeting there was a riot where all his equipment was destroyed, and he was stoned. The result was a total ban on all meetings of any kind outside the church or mosque compounds. The Muslim community became hostile and suspicious of all Christian activity. The visiting evangelist got some tremendous video footage for his television program back in Ireland and raised support because he was persecuted for the Gospel. His main accomplishment was destroying an ongoing lasting gospel witness in the community.

No matter where or when you share the gospel you must keep contextualization in mind. It is an issue that affects every area of communication in every area of life. Almost daily on the news and talk shows you hear people talk about something that was taken out of context. In other words, the job of contextualizing the message was not done properly.

To better understand this concept, I would recommend reading *The 3D Gospel* by Jayson Georges. This book seeks to teach primarily Western Christians how to contextualize the gospel, so that it is great news to all cultures.[xxxii] The Gospel of Jesus Christ is good news for every culture and can be contextualized so that people understand and accept it. Too many times church planters assume that everyone thinks the same way they do. Church planters must be students of the worldview of the people God has called them to. Jayson Georges writes about three basic "responses to sin found in human cultures: guilt, shame, and fear". From these responses come three basic worldviews of the Majority World cultures.

- the guilt-innocence worldview (mostly Western; individualistic societies).

- the shame-honor worldview (mostly in the East; collectivistic mindset).

- the fear-power worldview (typically tribal or African; referring to animistic cultures).[xxxiii]

In the western world, we tend to see things as black and white or as Jayson Georges would say as guilt and innocence. Therefore, most of our witnessing is based on the premise that people are guilty of sin and Jesus came to remove the guilt and restore their innocence. While living in East Africa we found this approach did not get the attention of most of the people. Much of Africa has a fear-power worldview so we presented the gospel message by saying that Jesus came to save mankind and give him power to be free from the fear and power of evil spirits. Now that we are living in an Arab country, we understand the shame-honor worldview. Here the gospel is presented by explaining how we have brought shame upon ourselves by disobeying the commandments of God. Jesus came to redeem us back to God by restoring our honor and removing our shame. Each of these three worldviews can be reached with the gospel with many scriptural texts for a foundation. In chapter 5 of *The 3D Gospel* you will find several good examples of presenting the gospel to these three different groups.

Michael Frost gives a wonderful explanation of three different positions when dealing with contextualization. Frost's three position are: Gospel-Over-Context Position, Context-Over-Gospel Position, and Gospel-In-Context Position.[xxxiv]

Briefly we will look at each of these three positions. There are more than these three, but these are the ones that are held by many church leaders, churches, and mission agencies around the world.

The Gospel Over Context Position believes the gospel is the only important thing. Any contextualization is a watering down of the gospel and should be avoided at all cost. Frost states, "Basically these people believe that an axiom like sola scriptura is synonymous with dogmatic theology, and that contextualization represents a compromise on the authority, uniqueness and sufficiency of Scripture."[xxxv]

The Context Over Gospel Position believes the context is the only thing that is important. The gospel can be compromised to any extent, so it becomes acceptable to the people you are trying to reach. In Africa you see some that accept forms of idol worship in their churches because it helps the people accept what they teach. Frost puts it this way, "What they hold in common is the need to respect, sometimes even to absolutize, the existing cultural context to the point where the gospel becomes distorted or where it assumes a subservient role.[xxxvi]

The Gospel In Context position believes the Gospel and context are important. Both should be understood so the gospel can be presented in a meaningful manner. Frost makes this observation, "Most people who take this third position could be classified as progressive evangelicals. They are committed to critical contextualization."[xxxvii]

It has been commonly reported that Francis A. Schaeffer, noted lecturer and author from *L'Abri* Fellowship in Switzerland, once said if he had only one hour to share the gospel with a person, he would spend the first forty-five minutes finding out what the person believed about God and the last fifteen minutes presenting Christ from that basis.[xxxviii]

Church planters would be wise to follow the advice of Francis A. Schaeffer. The more time spent in learning about a person's culture and worldview the better prepared one is to share the gospel. Rather than trying to "westernize" the unreached we need to "un-westernize the gospel".

Contextualization can be seen throughout the Bible. The most prominent proponent of contextualization is Paul. A study of the ministry of Paul reveals to us his message and his method changed to fit the situation and the audience. It was Paul who penned the words in 1 Corinthians 9:22 "To the weak I became as the weak, so that I might gain the weak. I am made all things to all *men*, so that I might by all means save some." The best example of Paul using contextualization is found in Acts 17:22 and 23. In the city of Athens Paul preaches and tells the people he saw a statue to the "Unknown God" and he has come to make that god known to them. Paul used something the people knew to share the gospel with them.

Michael Depew made the following comments about Paul's use of contextualization in Athens.

Paul had to convince them that Jesus was not just the Jewish Messiah, but he was a savior for the whole world. The Jewish Messiah seemed to them to be just that, the JEWISH Messiah. They had no Scriptures from god to depend on, they did not have the covenant relationship that the Jews had. They were not the "Children of the Covenant". But they were not without a witness. They were the "Children of Creation". The fact that God's hand could be seen in nature and the fact that they craved someone or something to worship pointed to a God who desired that kind of relationship. They knew that there was a God, but they needed guidance. This was the God that Paul preached to them, The God of creation, The God who had made them and everything around them. The God that sent the rains and the harvest. The God that they were to worship. Paul used what they knew about God and changed it. He modified their conception from an impersonal essence to the personal, living God of the Universe, and introduced them to the God of the Bible.[xxxix]

While living in Northeastern Kenya a very arid area the nomadic people we were trying to reach had no concept of snow. The statement that the blood of Jesus washes your sin as white as snow meant nothing to them. There is a washing powder called OMO with the slogan nothing washes whiter than OMO. To contextualize the scripture, we would say the blood of Jesus washes your sin whiter than OMO. They immediately understood the concept of be cleansed from their sin.

As Paul Little said in his book, *How To Give Away Your Faith*, "If we want to be effective in communicating the Gospel of Jesus Christ to others, we need to know how it is relevant to us personally. Then we must consider how to relate the relevant realities of Jesus Christ, including events that occurred two thousand years ago, to life in the twentieth century."[xl]

Redemptive Analogies

Don Richardson defined the concept of redemptive analogy in his books *Peace Child. Lords of the Earth, and Eternity in Their Hearts.* In *Peace Child* he began referring to the use of the Sawi peace-making ritual as a "redemptive analogy." He encouraged missionaries around the world to look for cultural rituals, folk beliefs, and tribal tales in which could be seen some parallel to crucial elements of the gospel. As Don Richardson reflected on the "redemptive analogy" concept, he became convinced that cultures everywhere contained starting points for gospel proclamation. Such thinking, of course, very much reflects the time-honored strategy of using the known to teach the unknown.[xli]

Of course, the idea was not really new. Jesus used the technique all the time in his storytelling: "The kingdom of God is like ..." Many of the prophets used it too, and preachers down the years. The gospel stories are so familiar to us, that we completely overlook the fact that Jesus' method of communication was totally revolutionary.

The New Testament approach is to communicate by way of redemptive analogy. Consider these examples:[xlii]

- The Jewish people practiced lamb sacrifice. John the Baptist proclaimed Jesus as the perfect, personal fulfillment of that sacrifice by saying, "Behold the Lamb of God, who takes away the sin of the world!" This is redemptive analogy.

- When Jesus spoke to Nicodemus, a Jewish teacher, both knew that Moses had lifted a serpent of brass upon a pole so that Jews, dying of snakebite, could look at it and be healed. Jesus told Nicodemus that "as Moses lifted up the serpent in the wilderness, even so must the Son of Man be lifted up, that whoever believes in Him should not perish, but have everlasting life." This too is redemptive analogy.

- A Jewish multitude, recalling that Moses provided miraculous manna on a six-day-a-week basis, hinted that Jesus ought to repeat His miracle of the loaves and fishes on a similar schedule. Jesus replied, "Moses gave you not the true bread from heaven. The true bread from heaven is He who comes down from heaven and gives life to the world...! am that Bread of Life!" Once again, redemptive analogy.

- When some charged that Christianity was destroying Jewish culture, the writer of the Epistle to the Hebrews showed how Christ actually fulfilled all the central elements of Jewish culture—the priesthood, tabernacle, sacrifices, and even the Sabbath rest. We call these redemptive analogies because they facilitate human understanding of redemption. Their God-ordained purpose is to precondition the mind in a culturally significant way to recognize Jesus as Messiah. Outside of scripture, it appears that God's general revelation is the source of redemption.

Chapter 5
Strategy: The Implementation of Missions

Definition of Strategy

Church planting begins in the heart and the will of God, yet it must function within different cultures and situations. Therefore, strategy is defined as *the practical working out of the will of God within a cultural context.*[xliii]

Church planters must be students of culture and human behavior to be effective in their mission of taking the Gospel to the ends of the earth. By working with national indigenous leaders, church planters are able to develop strategies which are not only based on the Word of God but are also culturally relevant. The church planter is not to impose his plan on the indigenous leaders but is to work with them to see how he can help them implement a strategy to share the gospel.

Missiology is made up of three interdependent areas of study: Theology, the Social Sciences, and Strategy. To facilitate understanding, these disciplines are described separately, even though they are closely related in the actual practice of missions. Picturing the areas of study in tiers implies that some are foundational to others.[xliv]

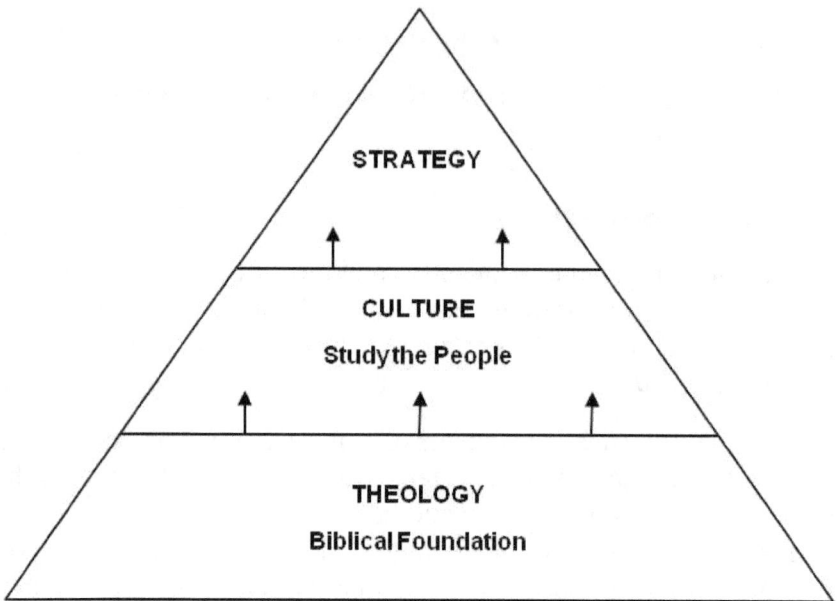

Chart of Church Planting

Our church planting must begin with the firm foundation of Biblical theology. Without a firm Biblical foundation our church planting structure will not stand. Through an understanding of the Word of God the church planter can see and feel the heart of God for the lost. The foundation of good Biblical theology is grounded on passages like John 3:16, "For God so loved the world that He gave His only-begotten Son, that whoever believes in Him should not perish but have everlasting life."

Once the Biblical foundation is laid (i.e. theology is correct) the worker must begin to seriously study the people and their culture. Questions must be asked to determine how the gospel fits into the local culture. What are the "cultural hooks" the gospel can be hung upon. The church planter must understand one of the major aspects of our church planting work is an understanding of local culture. Is there a redemptive analogy within the culture that will make presenting the gospel culturally relevant?

Finally, after the theological foundation is laid and there is an understanding of the local culture the church planting strategies can be set forth. Setting strategy without understanding the biblical foundation and the local culture is like having a car with no engine. It may look good, but it will not get the job done. Church planting strategy is built upon the foundation of God's Word. Once the foundation is solid the next layer to be built is a comprehensive understanding of the local culture. Then and only then can an effective church planting strategy be developed.

It is imperative for church planters to be faithful students of God's word and the local culture where they will minister. This is like a three-legged stool. For the stool to be effective all three legs must be in place.

Church Planter Training

The remainder of this chapter is based on the Church Planter training that was used by our team in West Africa while I was part of the Global 12 Project. Thousands of new churches were planted from the years 2000-2010 using this material to train church planters. Global 12 Project partnered with local churches to train their church planters, help them plant their church and give oversight, together with the sending pastor, to the church plant for one year. At the end of the first year the oversight of the new church was transferred from the Global 12 project to the local sending church. This was done because in many nations it is hard to get a new church registered with the government and the new church plant needs a local covering to operate.

Strategy – The "Micro-church"

The church planting strategy used in this training uses small groups to establish new churches in area where there are no churches. This strategy is known as the micro-church movement. A micro-church has several characteristics that make them unique.[xlv]

- Micro-churches have only a minimal amount of structure and just enough to allow them to function. Their organization tends to be flat as opposed to hierarchical, with a more egalitarian operation.

- At micro-churches people minister to one another and serve as priests to each other, as we find described in the New Testament.

- Micro-churches embrace the priesthood of all believers. This means that the people in the community minister to one another, teach one another, and help one another.

- The micro-church doesn't place as much emphasis on a Sunday morning service as traditional churches do. At micro-churches, weekly church gatherings prepare people to go into their community to serve.

- The micro-church has a vision to serve. Their mission is not inwardly focused but outwardly focused. Their internal gatherings, be it like a Sunday service or something else, are to encourage and prepare the people present to go out into their community and serve.

- The micro-church isn't concerned with growing its numbers, but it's vitally interested in growing influence. Micro-churches seek to do this by helping others start their own micro-churches to address other needs in the community. Their simple structure makes this easy and fast. They are constantly growing, changing, and reproducing more of their kind.

What Can We Achieve Together?

<u>The Dream Is Becoming a Reality!</u>

For the dream to become a reality there needs to be established church planting movements with the goal of working in teams to reach the unreached and neglected peoples of the world! We must have a commitment to team ministry. We will increase our success rate of planting many churches exponentially through partnership.

Working Together to Form the Network

Coming together is the beginning. Staying together is progress. Working together is success.[xlvi]

This popular quote is true! We have come together for a great eternal purpose. Let us determine to stay together and work together and God will grant us success. To function in a church planting movement, you must commit to working in a team and to recruiting new team members.

What is Expected of You?

We all have a network of personal relationships with pastors who should be interested in reaching the unreached and neglected areas of their nation. We hope that you will contact them and motivate them to do their part.

"From Him the whole body, joined and held together by every supporting ligament, grows and builds itself up in love, as each part does its work." Ephesians 4:16

Working Together to Plant Churches in Unreached Areas

The church planting movement leadership team will provide the focus and direction of where to plant micro-churches among the neglected and unreached peoples of your nation. But each church planter must also help identify the unreached and neglected peoples and areas and provide the core leadership.

Here are some guidelines when seeking a new church plant location among the unreached and neglected peoples of a nation. Invest time in analyzing, praying, and contemplating this exercise. The more time you invest, the better will be the result.

Selecting a Target Area

- List at least 5 potential areas/locations for a new church among unreached and neglected peoples in your area (from a database or locations you already know).

- Prioritize the list according to the *planned targeted growth* and goals of your specific team, and your sending church.

- Write out a list of advantages and disadvantages for the five areas/locations on your list.

- Discuss your strategy with your team leader.

- Research the possibilities of planting a new church in one or two of the areas. Remember, do not look at what you do not have, but look at what you have.

- Pray until you feel a release about one area.

- Select your church plant area.

Planting the Church

- Participate in the training programs that exist in your church.

- Make the final selection of the area in which you will plant a church.

- Attend a Church Planting Seminar.

- The candidate selects a mentor (preferably the sending pastor)

- Plant the new church

- Continue your part in supporting the planting of other churches

Implementation – How We Do It

Step 1: Intercession (Luke 10:2)

The objective of intercession is to open the spiritual doors of the city. Intercession must continue until you see the victory. A church planter must focus on intercession while he gains an understanding of the city (Step 2) and must continue with a focus on intercession until he establishes a relationship with a man of peace (Step 4). Of course, intercession should not end at that point, but the early stages of the church plant should see a focused attention on intercession.

There are two important aspects of embracing our priestly role that we want to examine. The first is *identification*, which is at the very heart of intercessory prayer. It is the ability and function of personally identifying with the needs of others to such an extent that in heart you become one of them by the Holy Spirit.[xlvii] There's more to identification than simply changing the pronouns from "them" to "us". Something much deeper is involved. (Daniel 9:15-19, and Nehemiah 1:3-11).

There are five essential requirements for this type of identificational intercession:[xlviii]

- People who are willing to look with their eyes open

- People who are willing to give up their lives

- A broken heart

- Grace to carry the burdens of others

- Desperate people willing to be the answers to prayers

A second aspect of priestly praying that we need to understand is the answer to this question: what happens in the Heavenlies when we pray? When we grasp the significance of this reality, it will charge your prayer life like few things could. We see from Revelations that our prayers to God are symbolically represented as incense before His throne room and altar in heaven. Let us look closely at Revelations 8:3-5.

> *Another angel, who had a golden censer, came and stood at the altar. He was given much incense to offer, with the prayers of all the saints, on the golden altar before the throne. The smoke of the incense, together with the prayers of the saints, **went up before God** from the angel's hand. The angel took the censer, filled it with <u>fire from the altar</u>, and **hurled it on the earth**; and there came peals of thunder, rumblings, flashes of lightening and an earthquake.*

Can you begin to see it? As Jim Goll concludes, what goes up must come down.[xlix] The angels take our prayers of intercession sent up before the throne, fill their censers with these prayers and *fire from the altar* in heaven, and cast them back down in signs and wonders upon the earth! Could this be why God is **looking** for people to stand in the gap? He is waiting to mix the prayers of the saints with fire from the altar and *send it back down* in power!

But there is more! Job 36:32 states that "God covers His hands with lightening, and commands it to *strike the mark*." The Hebrew word used here for "strike the mark" is the same word that is translated as "intercession" or "intervene" in Isaiah 59:16. Do you grasp this? Our intercession "marks the target" so that God's glory can strike the areas of need that we are praying for. Can you see this picture of God and His church of believer-priests working together to reach a people, put down injustice, destroy the works of the enemy, set free the captives, heal the sick and dying, and see the church released to be the beautiful bride that Jesus will receive? That is what happens when we pray. That is why we pray. That is what we were reborn to do!

Step 2: Understanding Your City (Luke 10:1)

Church Planting Movements have as a fundamental belief that Jesus desires to be in every city, town, and village. They also understand that the "Arm of God" that represents Jesus on earth is the Body of Christ, the church. After intercession, the second step is to understand the city or area to which Jesus has sent you. In truth, it can be said that you are gaining an understanding of the city while you invest time interceding. You need to continue to gain understanding and to have focused intercession until you find your "man of peace."

In practice, we intercede while we learn about a city, and we learn about a city when we intercede. One way to intercede for your city is to do a prayer walk. A prayer walk has three objectives:

- Putting our feet of conquest on the land

- Interceding before God for the land

- Gaining an understanding of the area

You will need to gain an understanding of the city and area in the following categories. Do not neglect to research the history of the community. That is critical in understanding why things are the way they are today. This process will take time and effort. But the more effort you give, the more targeted your church plant will be.

Understanding the Spiritual Environment

Matthew12:26 & 29 *"If Satan drives out Satan, he is divided against himself. How then can his kingdom stand? ... or again, how can anyone enter a strong man's house and carry off his possessions unless he first ties up the strong man? Then he can rob his house."*

Every location has its spiritual peculiarities. Every region is governed by spiritual powers that need to be identified and spiritually bound before we can "plunder" a city and bring to it the kingdom of God. Therefore we must first have an understanding of the spiritual environment.

Spiritual Mapping

1. Historical Survey

- The History of The City
  - o The Foundation of the City
  - o The Past History of the City
- The History of Religion in the City
  - o Non-Christian Religions
  - o Christianity
  - o Relationships amongst the various religions/ amongst believers/ divisions between denominations

2. Physical Survey:

- Who were the city planners; were any of them involved in the occult?

- Are there any significant designs and symbols embedded in the original plans or blueprints of the city?

- Is there any significance in the architecture, in relationship to the layout and positions of the main buildings?

- What is the background and possible significance of the statues and monuments of the city? Do any of them reflect demonic characteristics, glorifying creation, rather than glorifying the Creator

- What other objects of art appear in the city, especially in the public buildings, museums, and theaters? Search specifically for sensual and demonic objects of art.

- Where are the centers of highly visible sin, such as abortion clinics, pornographic bookstores or theaters, strip bars, gambling centers, bars, homosexual activities, etc.?

- Where are the areas that have a high concentration of lustful activities, exploitation, poverty, discrimination, violence, sickness, or frequent accidents?

- Are there any locations where blood was shed in the past or present, by means of massacres, wars or assassinations?

- Does the position of trees, columns, rocks, or rivers form any known and significant design or symbol?

3. Spiritual Survey

- Non-Christian

  o What are the names of the heavenly principalities or territorial spirits associated with the past or present of the city?

  o Where are the locations of the high places, altars, temples, monuments, or buildings associated with witchcraft, the occult, psychics, Satanism, Masons, Mormonism, oriental religions, Jehovah Witnesses, and other similar occults?

  o What are the places that in the past there was some kind of pagan worship even before the city was founded?

  o What are the different cultural centers that might contain objects of art or artifacts connected to pagan worship?

  o Is there any leader of the city, who being aware of the above might have dedicated himself or herself to any of them?

  o Have there been any known curses cast by the original inhabitants against the land or against those who founded the city?

- Christian

  - How have the messengers of God been received in the city?

  - Has the evangelization of the city been easy or difficult?

  - Where are the churches located and which ones do you see as life giving?

  - Are the churches of the city spiritually healthy?

  - Who are the evangelical leaders considered as elders of the city?

  - Is it easy for someone to pray anywhere in the city?

  - What is the condition of unity among the evangelical leaders regarding the question of ethnicity and denominationalism?

  - What is the opinion of the leaders of the city regarding Christian morals?

Identifyers:

- Mature intercessors that hear the voice of God in regard to the city.

- The identity of the principalities that seem to have total control of the city or specific areas of people's lives or over certain parts of the city.

Basic Principles For Mapping

- Rule 1: The Area - Select a geographic area that you can control, with discernable spiritual boundaries

- Rule 2: The Pastors - Assure the unity between pastors and other evangelical leaders of the region and begin to pray together regularly

- Rule 3: The Body of Christ - Project a clear mental image that the effort is not an activity solely of the Pentecostals and Charismatics, but the whole Body of Christ

- Rule 4: The Spiritual Preparation - Assure the spiritual preparation of the participating leaders and other believers by means of repentance, humility, and holiness.

- Rule 5: The Search - Search the historical background of the city, to determine what spiritual forces gave form to the city.

- Rule 6: The Intercessors - Work with a group of intercessors specifically called and anointed to engage in a strategic level of spiritual warfare to discover the divine revelation concerning these points: (a) The spiritual rulers of the city; (b) the satanic strongholds of the city; (c) the governing spirits designated by Satan over the city; (d) the collective sins of the past and present that need to be resolved; (e) the plan of attack and the opportune time determined by God

It is valuable to give a word of caution when dealing with a new location. New locations generally contain new spirits which you are not accustomed to confronting. This is very similiar to dynamics in the natural.

For example, when the Europeans came to colonize the new world, they brought with them diseases common in Europe, like the flu. Europeans, who were accustomed to the flu, rarely died from this illness. The Native Americans, on the other hand, did not have immunities to fight against viruses like the flu, and they died in great numbers until their bodies had built up antibodies against such viruses.

In the same manner, we must be conscience of the spiritual attacks that are certain to occur.

Understanding the Cultural Environment

There is nothing that irritates people more than strangers entering the city trying to change the culture without first seeking to understand the culture. We must understand the priorities, pride and even the personality of the culture in order for us to enter the lives of the people, even if the culture is based on doctrinal error.

Every area has its own peculiar culture. Recently a friend went to a small city that calls itself the "Worldwide Capital of Cachaça (a kind of liquor)." Obviously, this was a terribly bad title, but for the people of the city it was a great source of pride. An important factor in planting a church is to perceive that each city or region has to be treated uniquely, setting our aim on conquering the hearts of the people. Paul capitalized on this when he used the normal customs of the people of Athens to discuss new ideas in the public forum.

> *"All the Athenians and the foreigners who lived there spent their time doing nothing but talking about and listening to the latest new ideas."* Acts 17:21

Understanding the Practical and Social Environment

A significant part of planting a church is to meet practical needs in the community. If you do this, you will create an "open door" to the hearts of the residents. Can you name five practical and social needs of the community? Make an effort to meet with community leaders and longtime residents. Ask them about the community needs. Take what you learn and consider how your new church can address some of the needs in a significant manner. Share about your desire to plant a church and to serve the community. Pray for these individuals. Perhaps one of them will be your man of peace.

Rick Warren, author of the books "The Purpose Driven Church" and "The Purpose Driven Life," says that he started his church by doing a house to house survey asking three basic questions:

- What is the greatest need of this community?

- Who is working to meet this need?

- What could an evangelical church do to minister to this community?

Step 3: Define Your Values and Mission

After getting to know your community you are ready to begin defining your values and mission. Ralph Moore, the founder of a church-planting movement of more than 200 churches in three continents, suggests that value statements can be used as a blueprint and teaching tool for your new church[1]. You should display them publicly. The statements will answer the questions of, "*Why* do we do this or that?" Moore recommends that you develop up to 10 or 12 value statements like the examples shown in the previous session on values. These statements will be the foundations for the mission statement that you will develop. Frequently refer to your value statements in the months ahead as well as when you encounter ministry decisions. They will help you to stay on target.

At this point you can develop a mission statement, building upon God's vision for the target community and your values. *Because in truth, mission is determining how we can partner with God to see His vision come to pass.* Like your value statements, your mission statement will be used to filter your plans and decisions for the church-plant.

Church planting is people-driven; it is redemptive in nature. Its goal is to redeem people for God's glory. Unlike your value statements (which focused on the "whys"), your mission statement is *action oriented.* Mission is about the people that God has called you to serve and reach. To understand your mission, you must answer three questions:[li]

- WHOM are you called to reach?

- WHAT are the needs that you are able to meet?

- HOW will you meet those needs?

Here is an example of a non-church mission statement. Can you identify the "who, what and how" of this statement? Notice that this mission statement is not overly detailed yet provides a concise and descriptive explanation of how it will *address the needs* of the target audience. The details of the "how" will be defined later.

The Southshore Medical Center exists to provide the emergency medical needs of the southern metropolitan area of River City by providing 24 hour affordable, efficient, and caring urgent care services.

Ideally, you want to express all three components of your mission (who, what, how) into a sentence of 25 words or less. However, if you wish, begin by putting your mission into a brief paragraph. You can summarize it into a sentence later. Also, you will want to develop a popularized version or slogan of your mission statement, a "bumper sticker" version. Then put that on all your promotional materials!

Step 4: Finding a "Man of Peace"

> *"If a man of peace is there, your peace will rest on him; if not, it will return to you. Stay in that house, eating and drinking whatever they give you, for the worker deserves his wages. Do not move around from house to house."*
> Luke 10:6-7

Perhaps the most important step in planting a church is finding a man of peace. The verse above is many times misunderstood. Many think that only the church planter blesses the house and the owner with his peace, but in truth it is the owner that gives a place for the church planter or worker to rest in peace. In this way, all are blessed, the worker and the owner and the community.

In our experience and research, we understand that all successful churches have a man (or woman) of peace. This person is generally someone prepared in advance by God to be a source of peace for the new pastor. In the Bible, a good example of a woman of peace was Mary, who brought peace to Jesus while he was ministering to the needs of the many.

> *"There were also women looking on afar off: among whom was Mary Magdalene, and Mary the mother of James the less and of Joses, and Salome; Who also, when he was in Galilee, followed him, and ministered unto him; and many other women which came up with him unto Jerusalem."* Mark 15:40-41

Some characteristics of a man of peace are:

- He sees the new pastor as his pastor and comes under his authority

- He is in the church from the beginning

- He makes available his resources without expecting anything in return

- He upholds the vision of the pastor as if it were his

- He is someone that many times is unknown to the congregation and remains behind the scenes as a support.

It is imperative that a new pastor establishes a relationship of discipleship with the man of peace. Do not let the man of peace become the owner of the vision. His role is to be a source of stability and peace for the new pastor. The new pastor, at the same time, has to recognize that the man of peace has been a great blessing given by God to the new church up to this point.

Initiate a discipleship relationship with him/her:

- Deal with areas of his life bringing healing to any wounds in order that he can be an effective worker

- Permeate him with your vision, excitement, and passion for the new church

- Fill him with the love for souls, specifically for his friends, family, and others that he knows that do not have a relationship with Jesus.

Step 5: Evangelize People Who Are Close to Your Man of Peace

"Again, I tell you that if two of you on earth agree about anything you ask for, it will be done for you by my Father in heaven. For where two or three come together in my name, there I am with them." Matthew 18:19-20

As soon as a man of peace is located, you could say that the church has been initiated. Indeed, this is a day of celebration because the church can now move into the next phase of development. With a man of peace, you have:

- The beginning of a team for evangelization

- A family to win to the Lord, a neighborhood to win to the Lord

- An area of the city to win to the Lord

- Professional relationships and friends to begin evangelizing

The man of peace is the initial focus of all relationships of the church and is also the beginning of a network of relationships that will become part of your team that will launch the celebration service. This is key because there is much work to be done before you are ready to launch the services. Focus all your energies on evangelizing the new relationships brought through the man of peace.

Rick Warren, pastor, and author of the book "The Purpose Driven Church," says that a new pastor should set a goal to personally reach the first 100 members of the church. This sets the example for the members. You are still in the phase of focusing on evangelization, and now there are people on whom you can concentrate your energies. Remember, the first 100 members of your church will determine the next 300.

As soon as possible, you must organize an encounter retreat to bring healing to the new members of the forming cell. The encounter can be done with another church, but this is not necessary. A smaller encounter led by the pastor is a great start if the new members cannot travel a great distance. Do not worry about starting small. After the encounter, they must be discipled with the aim to connect them with the new pastor and church. Some churches call this the post-encounter. The objective of this is to consolidate or unite the church. A secondary objective is to strengthen the connection with the man of peace. If friends and members of his family are being ministered to by the church, the man of peace will also be connected with them.

Step 6: Initiating the Cells and Forming a Team

"Who despises the days of small beginnings?" Zechariah 4:10

Form a Team

Executing an excellent celebration service requires many people who are trained well. You need people for a worship team, to care for the children, activities, consolidate visitors, do the sound, etc. For all this the pastor needs a team. This team must be formed from the members of your first cells.

The first cell must be led by the pastor. Within this cell discipleship occurs. Most of the discipleship that Jesus did took place while the disciples were talking with and working alongside of Him. Your first cell must function in the same manner.

Create a System for Training

Every church must create a system to train leaders. This system must have two components of discipleship: individual and corporate.

Individual Discipleship

Jesus invested much of His time in a few people. However, these few people won and consolidated thousands of souls for the kingdom. This kind of discipleship is best developed through the cell and then the group of 12.

Corporate Discipleship

When a church is still small (less than 40 people), all the discipleship can be done individually by the new pastor and his wife. However, as soon as there is sufficient leadership available, corporate discipleship becomes necessary.

Corporate discipleship is a system of training workers or new cell leaders. Some call this the School of Leaders. This system equips each member with the tools to become an effective leader. It also provides the quality control that cells are functioning correctly. For example, a person that enters the school of leaders is learning how a cell should operate. If he informs the instructor that the cell in which he is a member is not operating correctly, the instructor can use this information to bring correction to the cell leader.

Step 7: Plan Your Finances

Assumption of Provision

We want to begin this session with a great word of encouragement – *your new church will always have enough finances to fulfill God's call*. Why? Because the Word of God says so! "He will supply all your needs from his glorious riches, which have been given to us in Christ Jesus" (Phil. 4:19). Let us take God at His word and *assume that His provision will always be adequate*. Take to heart these words of experience from Ralph Moore.[lii]

"I have found that an apparent absence of resources <u>always</u> <u>stimulates better vision</u>. When this happens, <u>I assume that I am</u> <u>missing something good</u> that God has already made available. Prayer, Bible study, deep conversations and an understanding of the technical world help me when I reach this point. These factors collaborate to stimulate whatever new direction God is trying to communicate."

Opportunity Versus Operational

With God's promises in mind, let us turn to the financial planning of the church plant. The key is not to make a budget, but to make *two* budgets – an opportunity budget and an operational budget. They are different in function, and you should approach them from vastly different angles. An operating budget allows you to plan and control recurring costs of ministry. An opportunity budget covers one-time opportunities that are especially related to starting a church with momentum. What are included in the budgets?

Operating Budget

- Pastor's salary and benefits, if applicable

- Paid support staff (usually part-time), if applicable

- Rent for your meeting place

- Office rent, if applicable

- Utilities – telephone, internet, water, etc.

Opportunity Budget

- Outreach activities

- Core-team meetings

- Opening day functions

- Banners, signs, brochures, etc.

- Sound system

- Chairs and other furniture for service

- Equipment for children's and youth ministries

- Advertising and promotion

- Communication system sufficient to operate the church by a team of volunteers

Your objective with these two budgets is clear. ***Your goal is to limit your operating budget as much as possible so that you can capitalize on opportunities.*** This is the best way for your budget to contribute to church growth.

Review your church start-up needs. Attach a cost estimate as necessary to each ministry need. Project all expenses through the *first year* of the church. Separate all the costs and list them into two columns on a sheet of paper – one for opportunities, the other for operational costs. ***Try to find creative ways to shift funds from operations to opportunity***.

Biblical Financial Principles for Growth

- Look for outside financial help only as needed.

- End outside funding early. Outside sources can especially help with initial opportunity costs. Dependency on outside sources for operational costs for more than about a year or so is not healthy for the new church.

- *Give while you are receiving!* Give generously as a church to others. Make a point to instill generosity into the congregation for the purposes of the kingdom. *What could you do in the first month to inject a spirit of generosity into the church?*

- Never beg for money.

- Be positive about money. *Report results not just need!*

- *Teach giving tithes and offerings.* If you do not, you will have an anemic church because people will not be living under God's blessing. Sometimes let church leaders (not staff) teach about the tithes and offerings.

Step 8: Finding a Meeting Location

Everyone reading this would agree that the church is not a building. Starting the church with a small building of your own really is not a necessity. In fact, having such a facility can limit the growth of your new church rather than help.

Some cities may have government or private infrastructure in which a temporary facility may be rented for just your services rather than renting a facility 24 hours a day, seven days a week.[liii] These could be a school, cinema, public recreational facility or even a town hall. Many great churches around the world started in facilities rented just for the services. Today these churches have congregations of thousands.

Here are several reasons why you may want to consider *temporary facilities just for your services.*

Benefits of Temporary Facilities

- It allows flexibility. Buildings shape *your* thinking. Most often they restrict rather than liberate you. A church could outgrow its meeting place several times in just one year.

- It eliminates major capital outlay. Buildings require rent and additional services such as cleaning and security. Try to rent space for the *few hours a week* that you have services. Plus, *consider not buying land or a building for at least five years.* This is good stewardship of your resources.

- It reduces distractions. A property acquisition, construction or remodeling program always shifts attention away from evangelism and discipleship.

- It keeps expectations in check. A series of rented facilities can keep members, and visitors, happier than a semi-permanent location! Why? It is because short-term facilities *feel* temporary. People stay more focused on the growth of the ministry rather than the conditions of the bathrooms and the color of the walls. There is a sense that the future will be bigger and better.

- It provides easy entry into ministry responsibilities. There is a benefit for stacking the chairs and packing up the equipment after every service. You can recruit new people, even non-Christians, to take part in helping. It gives even first-time visitors a chance to help and gives you an opportunity to see who the people are willing to serve, even without asking.

- You can establish the functions of an office elsewhere. An office provides communications, storage, meeting space and a mailbox. Find a way to supply each function without renting for as long as you can. *Spend your money on technology rather than rent as long as possible.*

What to Look for In a Meeting Space

What should you look for in a meeting space? First, look for an accessible site, one that is not hard to find. The more accessible, the better. Roy Stockstill, founder of Bethany World Prayer Center once said as soon as you need to put up a sign pointing to were the church is, then you really should be putting the church were the sign is. It is true that the location of a cell church is not as important as for a traditional church, but attention should be given to practical aspects also. Areas where people in streets, pathways, and public squares congregate are obviously preferential locations to start a new work.

Second, consider the size of the meeting space. It is better to be in a place that feels a bit too small than one with large empty areas. A packed meeting may help to build excitement in what God is doing. Plus, you can always double your meeting space by adding a second meeting. And third, try to find a building with "soul", that little something that makes it special. If there is a choice in locations, opt for the one that gets people talking.

*Here are some **guidelines** for renting a meeting location.*

- First, list at least 10 potential meeting locations for a new church in your target community. Be creative and think outside the box.

- Second, prioritize the list according to the *planned growth* of your church. This will give you a head start for the future.

- Third, write out a list of advantages and disadvantages for the first five locations on your list.

- And fourth, research the possibilities of renting those five facilities.

- Remember this final word of wisdom from Ralph Moore; *"We control the initial decision as to where we will meet. But from that point on, <u>our location controls us</u>. Be sure you are controlled in a manner that ensures rather than hinders growth."[liv]*

Step 9: Making Your Church Known in the Community

At this point, let us remind ourselves that the heart of church planting is reaching non-Christians (or shall we say pre-Christians). Your goal is to connect with your target community. Consider the following statement.

"Reaching pre-Christians is an intentional process. There is nothing accidental about it. Connecting with pre-Christians in

*your community must be **a core value if you are going to accomplish your mission**. It must be a value shared by your launch team.* "[lv]

Regardless of your church structure or ministry model, outreach usually involves all three of the following activities:

- Personal relationships

- Ministering to community needs

- Public visibility

Please understand that you do not need to wait for your launch date to begin some of these activities. Specifically discuss with your team what can be done before the launch. Let us take a brief look at each of the three types of outreach.

First, we all have a network of personal relationships. Make a list of names including: 1) people you come in contact with regularly, 2) people you plan to or already have initiated a relationship with, 3) people in your circle of interaction because of another relationship, and 4) people who have expressed an interest in spending time with you. Pray regularly for these people. Choose at least three names that you can prayer for in Prayers of Three. Share your vision for the Prayer of Three with your cell, team, and man of peace. This will encourage them to do the same. Expect God to move and step out in faith. And, *have a plan to equip your team to be "inviters."*

Second, there are the community needs that you have already identified. You and your team can begin some formal or informal activities to address a need even before the church begins. Consider what your team can begin now. This is a great opportunity to begin serving the community and touching the lives of pre-Christians. *It will help build the momentum of the church leading up to the launch date.*

Third, is public visibility, which is mostly comprised of publicity. Consider carefully what materials will best raise the visibility of your church – *be creative*. You must consider three things about publicity: time, costs and needed expertise. Beyond conventional advertising, consider what public events, activities, or community service your team can do that will "get people talking" about your new church. *These activities can be much more effective and usually less expensive.*

Step 10: Begin the Services

Once people initially connect to your church by participating in a church function, are they going to have a meaningful experience? Will it be enough to bring them back? Statistics show that even with three visits, they only have about a 50% chance of joining your church. This step focuses on your primary service, although informal contact with new people is just as important for creating meaningful experiences for them.

Have a Preaching Plan

Do you have a preaching plan to kick-off the church? You need to have one! You will be so consumed with the details and new people in the early stages of the church plant that the ministry of the Word will suffer if you are not prepared. The church needs a strong foundation, and that will largely come from your teaching of the Bible. You should consider some teaching series or even periodically teaching through a book of the Bible. This models for your members how they can study the Bible and creates stability in the congregation. Make it fun! You can even create banners or posters to promote an upcoming teaching series. Let it touch the "heartbeat" of the community.

Ralph Moore suggests that you have a preaching plan for the first *two years* of the church. This is his plan. First, he teaches through the book of Philippians in four weeks. This is a crowd gathering time. Next is the book of Acts, which teaches a pattern for church, evangelism, and world vision. Next, he moves into Romans and forms a theological foundation and teaches about spiritual gifts. He finishes with I Corinthians, which deals with love, unity, and power. Make a plan that fits you *but make a plan*. As Ralph Moore says, "Your teaching strategy should *set your vision in the context of New Testament life and evangelism*, much like a jeweler would center a fine diamond in a setting of golden splendor."[lvi]

Creating a Meaningful Worship Experience

Do you know who the worship leader is in every church? It is the pastor, even if he can't play an instrument or sing! The pastor must set the vision for the worship; then you can leave the music to the worship team. Utilize the following suggestions to help develop a meaningful worship experience in your church.

- It is better if you, the pastor, do not actually lead the worship. You want to show the congregation that you believe in team ministry. Plus, you want to delegate responsibility. Thus, this is a position you want in place before launch.

- Make sure the members of your worship team are worshippers, not just musicians.

- Remember that the members of the worship team are leaders and are viewed as such by the congregation. They must be fully participating in your vision as the pastor.

- Better to have a few quality musicians than a full band with weak musicians.

- As soon as possible, incorporate multiple members into you worship team so that there can be a rotation.

- If you build a worship team that embodies the local culture, you will own the hearts of the community.

Step 11: Serving the Community

The body of Christ is called to be the light of the world (Matthew 5:14). How did Jesus describe that light? We are to be a city on a hill that cannot be hidden. But does that mean He intended us to have a big building with loud music and many events in order that the community could not miss our church even if they tried? Not exactly. Jesus went on to explain, "Let your lights shine before men, that they may see your good deeds and praise your Father in heaven" (Matt. 5:16).

We can draw a few conclusions from this scripture. First, being a light for Jesus includes doing *good works* in our communities in addition to evangelizing. The early church in Acts obviously embraced this message as evident by their insistence to remember the poor. In our churches today we often call this "servant evangelism," which is fine. Too often, though, our servant evangelism becomes too "event oriented" and sporadic. *We would do a greater service to the community and make a greater impact if we would select one or two areas of need and consistently serve in that area.* Only in this manner can we make a significant difference.

Second, we need to make sure that we have the right motive when we serve. Jesus was clear. We are to do our good deeds so that the people will "glorify your Father who is in heaven." *Be careful that you do not view your service as another church growth effort.* Serving with a motive to receive something in return is not really serving at all. People will recognize your sincerity. When you serve and love without expectation of return, people will turn their lives over to God. God will bring the fruit to your church.

Step 12: Multiplication & Missions – Vision for Others

What is the fruit of your new church? Is it souls saved from the kingdom of darkness? Yes, but only partially. Like gives birth to like. People give birth to people; churches should give birth to churches. In all the details and effort of planting a church, you must keep one critical factor in the forefront – you want to begin this church as a reproducing church. Build it into the DNA of the church. Speak it and preach as often as you can, to yourself and others! Multiplying your church should probably be one of your value statements and perhaps part of your mission statement. If you do this, you and the church will not be content until you are planting other churches. Consider and implement three practical things that you could do to program the idea of multiplication into the mindset of the congregation from the outset.

You may be thinking about the timing of your first church multiplication. Although the timing must come from the Holy Spirit and be confirmed by your leader, here are two guidelines. First, if you have at least 120 people in your church, you should be about ready to plant another church. Second, if your church is at least five years old, you should have the capacity to plant another church. Leadership should be developed and ready to launch out. If you are pastoring a church right now that is over five years old and has at least 120 in attendance, it is time to plant another church!

And finally, as we have spoken about much already, your new church must be committed to missions. Missions is just sowing "beyond your field" with the intention to bless others without expecting return. You may spiritually cover this new church plant, but your goal is for them to be self-governing, self-sufficient and themselves with a vision to multiply in the same way. That is a healthy church. That is the church the way that Jesus designed it to be. That is the kind of church that we are committed to be.

Multiplication – Sending Your Best for the Harvest

Many times, things in the Kingdom of God are counterintuitive. Give and it shall be given to you, it is better to give than to receive, even, if someone asks you to carry a load for one mile, carry it two. In the same manner, the concept of sending your best is also counterintuitive.

We teach the church about principles of tithes and offerings, but many pastors do not live what they preach. So many times, pastors are stingy when it comes to sending their best people. We preach we should give our best to God. God is not a beggar that He should receive 'undesirables.' Yet, when we think about sending someone to bless someone else's vision, we hold back from sending our best and we simply send someone mediocre.

As pastors we think, we have invested years into discipling and training our workers. We invest our toil and tears in them. We help them through their most difficult times. When it is all said and done, how can they leave us? Aren't they our workers, our leaders, our associate pastors? Truly, we know that they are not ours, yet we feel like they are.

This session will focus on the principles of sowing under the context of human resources. However, the principles presented here are also valid for all other resources including finances.

We are Blessed

The Purpose of Blessings

> Genesis 18:18 *"...since Abraham will surely become a great and mighty nation, and in him all the nations of the earth will be blessed?"*

In the book of Esther, Mordecai said to Esther: "For if you remain silent at this time, relief and deliverance will arise for the Jews from another place and you and your father's house will perish. And who knows whether you have not attained royalty for such a time as this?" Esther 4:14

Peter Wagner once said that he thought Brazil would one day pass the USA in regards to the number of missionaries being sent. Could it be that God is placing Brazil in a position of blessing for an eternal purpose of His? Of course it is!

But just like Esther, there is just one window of opportunity before deliverance arises from another place. Esther acted.

A Window of Opportunity

In chapters 13 and 14 of Numbers we see a window of opportunity. God opened an opportunity for the Israelites to enter, conquer, and occupy the Promised Land. There was only one window of opportunity. After the window closed and the opportunity was lost the Israelites said, "In the morning, however, they rose up early and went up to the ridge of the hill country, saying, 'Here we are; we have indeed sinned, but we will go up to the place which the Lord has promised.' But Moses said, 'Why then are you transgressing the commandment of the Lord, when it will not succeed? Do not go up, lest you be struck down before your enemies, for the Lord is not among you.'" (Numbers 14:40-42).

We all know the story. The window of opportunity opened and then closed. When the people finally wanted to take advantage of the opportunity, it was closed. Even when they had all repented before the Lord, the window did not reopen. The window never reopened during their lifetime.

We believe that there is a window of opportunity for missions and church planting. Today is the day of salvation. The time for your church to launch and send has never been more ready than now. Let us sacrifice, invest, and assume the responsibility to reach the interior cities, even to the ends of the earth.

The Laws of Sowing

The Kingdom of God Functions According to Sowing and Reaping

Genesis 8:22 "While the earth remains, seedtime and harvest, and cold and heat, and summer and winter, and day and night shall not cease."

This law not only applies to farming but also to all areas of our lives. In Galatians 6:9, Paul wrote about this law applying it to our carnal nature and eternal life. Likewise, it is natural to expect that this law also applies in the area of church planting.

Seeds Produce Fruit After Their Kind

Genesis 1:12 "And the earth brought forth vegetation, plants yielding seed after their kind, and trees bearing fruit, with seed in them, after their kind; and God saw that it was good."

The verse above guarantees us an eternal principle. Everything that multiplies reproduces itself after its kind. This is a powerful truth, and should make us happy, but should also fill us with fear. What do you desire to reproduce? Your best, or your leftover? If we invest our leftovers, we will have a harvest of leftovers, but if we invest our best, we will have an abundant harvest.

There is a story about a young man named Edimilson who came to Rio de Janeiro from Paraiba, another state in a rural part of Brazil. He was born into a difficult life having to start working with his parents at the early age of 7. He had to stop studying and never was able to get past third grade, but what he learned from life with his father was of great benefit to him.

After the harvest, his father spent weeks separating the corn. He went through ear after ear of corn separating the best. He separated the small ears of corn and the ones that were rotten into one pile, and the big and perfect ears of corn into another pile. After all the ears were separated, Edimilson eagerly looked forward to tasting the big and perfect ones, and asked his father when they were going to have lunch so that they could enjoy the corn, pointing at the pile of big and perfect ears. But his father exclaimed back to him, "Never!" He explained that they would be eating the small and rotten ones. Then Edimilson asked if they were going to sell the good and perfect ears and his father once again exclaimed "Never!" His father continued to explain to him that the good and perfect ears would be saved to be used as seed for next year so that they would have a greater harvest. Edimilson tells this story saying that many times they went without food in their house, but his father preferred to go into town and buy corn at the market rather than to eat the corn separated for sowing.

This is how our attitude should be concerning our resources. Our leaders, members, and associate pastors in reality are not ours, but we are simply the caretakers of what belongs to God.

The Seed is in the Center of the Fruit

> Genesis 1:29   *"Then God said, "Behold, I have given plant yielding seed that is on the surface of all the earth, and every tree which has fruit yielding seed: it shall be for you"*

It is interesting to note that God said this to man while he was in paradise. When God said this to man, he had everything he needed. These words of God were the promise for sustaining him. Why then did God emphasize the seed?

The seed is the source of provision for tomorrow. So many times, we ask the Lord for provision, but the source of that provision is already in our hand. The seed is in the middle of the fruit.

Applying this law to human resources, we see that since the seed is found in the center of the fruit, it is logical that God expects us to send and sow our workers that are in the center of the vision of our church. Resist the temptation to only send workers that are on the periphery of what you are doing. Send your "right-hand man".

A Seed Must Die Before It Germinates

> John 12:24 *"Truly, truly, I say to you, unless a grain of wheat falls to the earth and dies, it remains by itself alone; but if it dies, it bears much fruit.*

Often, we are tempted to just give when we receive a benefit in return. We become guilty of trying to sow a seed and eat it at the same time. Jesus taught that the seed needs to die before it can bear fruit. The seed needs to die; it must leave our hand, our control. David said "No, but I will surely buy it from you for a price, for I will not offer burnt offerings to the Lord my God which cost me nothing." 2 Samuel 24:24

Sowing is Always a Painful Process

A seed can be eaten or sown. But a farmer who invests his seed is saying, "I am sowing something that is mine to eat, except for the promise of a greater return in the future."

The time for sowing is the most expensive part of the year for a farmer. He has to economize and save throughout the whole year to be able to buy the best and the greatest quantity possible of seeds. Look at the example of the Father who gave his only Son so that a marvelous harvest would be realized in us.

Sowing Has to be Important to You

> 2 Samuel 24:24 *However, the king said to Araunah, "No, but I will surely buy it from you for a price, for I will not offer burnt offerings to the LORD my God which cost me nothing." So David bought the threshing floor and the oxen for fifty shekels of silver.*

We never should give God our leftovers. The great testimonies of multiplication by God start with the question, "What do you have in your hand?"

- The widow with a little oil and flour made the first cake for Elijah

- Another widow gave the little oil she had left in a small vessel at the word of Elisha and paid off all her debts and lived well with what was leftover

- A small boy gave his bread and fish to the Lord, probably the food for his entire family

We are asking you today "What do you have in your hands that you can invest in the Kingdom of God"?

- Don't be afraid to invest your best

- Don't be afraid to invest in a vision that is beyond the scope of you own

- Don't be afraid to invest beyond your control

- Don't be afraid to sacrifice

Goals – Where Do We Go from Here?

EVANGELIZE

- Become a part of a team (receive and give mentorship) 40 days

- Form your Team in 40 weeks

- Identify the existing churches and leaders where you are and invite them to a church planting Seminar, Pastors' Breakfast, or simply form a relationship with them and at the appropriate time share about the unreached peoples your church planting movement is reaching. 40 days

- Motivate the members of your church to assume some responsibility together with you regarding new church plants, i.e. intercession, information gathering, raising resources, etc. 40 days

ESTABLISH

- Communication with mentor: _____ times per month

- Communication with team leader: _____ times per month

- Communication with team members: _____ times per month

- Identify the unreached and neglected peoples in a target area in 40 days

- Formulate your plan to plant a church in the target area in 40 weeks

EQUIP

- Train your best leaders in 40 weeks

- Train your potential leaders in 40 months (3.5 years)

EMPOWER

- Send your best leaders in 40 weeks

- Send your potential leaders in 40 months (3.5 years)

As a Team:

- Plant _____ New Churches in 40 weeks

- Plant _____ New Churches in 40 months (3.5 years)

Individually:

- Plant _____ New Churches in 40 weeks

- Plant _____ New Churches in 40 months (3.5 years)

PRAYER

- When man works, man works; when man prays, God works.

- We don't just pray for the work; Prayer is the work!

Prayer goals:

Personal: _____

Project Team: _____

Church: _____

Chapter 6
Church Planting

Traits of a Church Planter

We borrowed this excellent list from the www.mcflorida.org web site however this site is no longer available. If you are asking, do I have what it takes to plant a church? -- see if you can come up with specific examples of how you have demonstrated the behaviors below. Church Planters do not need to hit a home run in every category, but these are the overall traits of a planter.

- Clear visionizing capacity.... Can hear the will of God and communicate God's vision for the church to the people in such a way that the people of the church take personal ownership in the vision.

- Clear calling by God.... Knows that God has called them to this community to accomplish the Great Commission through people not to people.

- Empowering Leadership.... Can empower God's people to be an effective church that multiplies disciples. Creates ownership in ministry by the church.

- Community Involvement.... Is well connected in the non-churched community outside the church walls. Knows what the hot buttons of the community are and is able to take the gospel into the culture.

- Peer Relationships with the Unchurched.... follows closely with community involvement. Has friends that are at a peer level outside the church. Typically business people, sales persons, teachers, athletics, etc.

- Entrepreneur Ability... Able to start things from scratch. Either inside the church or in the business world.

- Passionate Spirituality.... Thinks Jesus is cool and knows that everyone else will too.

- Can Do Attitude.... Sees the glass as half full and on the way to the top.

- Resilience.... Sees obstacles as opportunities. Gets up and keeps going. When you hit the wall -- you find a ladder.

- Commitment to the Great Commission.... Has proven track record or making disciples that multiply other disciples. Also, honestly believes that people are going to spend eternity in hell if the church does not reach them.

Ten Commandments of Church Planting

There are some things that you must do for a successful mission.

- Pray, Pray, Pray

- Check Your Motives

- Let God Change You

- Desire to Learn, Stay Teachable

- Love People more than the Vision

- Preach Values before Vision

- Start Small

- Train Intentionally

- Eliminate Distractions

- Multiply Leaders

Types of People

WORLD A 24%

Those who have **never** heard the gospel of Jesus Christ with such cultural and personal relevance that it results in sufficient understanding to accept Christ by faith as a believer (disciple) or to reject Him. A people for which most of its members have little, or no, access to the gospel. There is no viable indigenous church movement with sufficient strength, resources, and commitment to sustain and ensure the continuous multiplication of churches. Less than 2% Christian.

WORLD B 42%

Those who **have heard** the gospel of Jesus Christ with such cultural and personal relevance that it results in sufficient understanding to accept Christ by faith as a believer (disciple) or to reject Him.

WORLD C 34%

Those who have made a personal profession of faith in Christ.

How to Identify the Unreached and Unsaved

There are two schools of missions in the church today. Most churches fit into one of these two.

Missions as a project – focuses on directing energy into vision trips, prayer walks, vacations with a purpose, designated projects and offerings, short term missions, and ministry teams. (Support projects and one-time needs)

Missions as a process – focuses on church planting, strategies, track records, doctrinal statements, and long-term associations. (Monthly support of veteran missionaries).

A third school of missions is rising these days that I hope all of us will be part of.

GET THE JOB DONE: A proper mission's vision should incorporate both aspects. We need the long-term commitment, but we also need the short-term trips to fire the people up. Paul said I become all things to all men that I might win a few. Do whatever God tells you to do when he tells you to do it and how he tells you to do it. (the lady standing on her head)

How to identify the unreached and unsaved people in your community, city, nation, continent, world.

Unsaved – those who have had a witness but have never given their heart to Jesus.

- The unsaved are those people who claim to be Christians but have never made a decision for Christ or those who are open to the Gospel message. They may be in your church, community, on the job, at school, etc.

  Unreached – those who have never had a gospel witness (not just hearing about Jesus)

- An unreached people group is any people who are less than 2% Christian and have no viable witness among them. They can be grouped by geographic divisions (North Africa, Francophone Nations, sections of your city), habitat (Mexico City dump dwellers, Nairobi street children, refugee camps), tribe (Fulani, Pygmy, Hausa) language (Korean, French, Swahili, German), religion (Islam, Buddhist, Witchcraft), common interest (dock workers, migrant laborers. ex-patriots).

We must make a distinction between the two groups, so we know the strategy to use to reach each group. The method for reaching each group is vastly different.

The unsaved will respond to traditional forms of evangelism (crusades, door to door, street meetings, etc.)

The unreached need a fresh approach – there is a reason that they are still unreached after 2000 years of church history (In Kenya the unreached tribes live in remote areas, the areas have lack of security and most of them are Muslims). There is a key to reach each people group. You must spend time in God's presence to discover the key. God knows the key to every lock.

10 Principles to Evangelize the Unreached

1. You Are The Key

- An indigenous church planting movement among every people must be the point of all we do.

- Plans, programs, and technology are not our foremost consideration but only means to the end.

- You, as a worker among unreached peoples (your competency and character), are the key in reaching the destination.

- Thus, we must do all we can to provide adequate support, training, and guidance.

2. We Must Continually Change

- The unreached world is an ever-changing world of governments and forces who are belligerently resisting Gospel witness.

- Our willingness to challenge and change the way we do things has been one of our chief strengths.

- Unwillingness to challenge what has become status quo or conventional wisdom will mean stagnation.

- Thus, we must continually check our course, making minor adjustments and even major changes.

3. Organizational Conformity for The Sake Of Conformity Is Death

- Our Lord has created something unique and distinctive in each of us -- for the sake of the nations.

- To sacrifice the nations on the altar of organizational expediency or uniformity is wrong.

- We are all part of a larger family, and yet, we do not have to look or act exactly like our brothers and sisters.

- Our motivation must not be conformity to organizational standards, procedures, and policies.

- Rather, our motives must be driven by what it will take to reach the nations, not by what it will take to strengthen the name of our organization.

4. We All Live Under Authority and Are Accountable.

- We live together under the covenant to bless the nations.

- In this relationship, we mentor, correct, teach, and support each other.

- Thus, all of us are accountable to someone in a linear, corporate-like structure where individuals under authority are empowered for appropriate decision-making and leadership.

- We don't take votes and we don't establish committees.

- The context in which we work and the stewardship of resources demand that we operate in the most efficient, effective manner possible.

5. The Way Forward Must Be Through Humility and Service.

- The vision and passion which we share for the nations and which we believe to be the very heart of our God will not be grasped by others through our arrogance or power of persuasion, but only through our humility and service to the rest of the Christian community.

- The politics of power and turf are not the way of our Lord, so they should not be our way either.

- We must continually remember that we participate in taking the Edge only at our Lord's gracious invitation.

6. Communication Must Be Wide and Secure

- We must redouble our efforts and use the latest means to communicate effectively and securely with each other and our constituency

7. The Greater Our Diversity, The Greater Our Strength

- A leveling of everyone to the lowest common denominator is not our aim.

- Everyone must not look and act the same.

- Equity is not our way of operating. Each of you will be treated differently.

- Our aim must be to maximize everyone's unique gifts and personality so that the destination is reached.

8. The Edge Is Where We Belong.

- As individuals and as a group, we dare not draw back from the Edge of the unreached.

- We are people who are gifted for and called to the Edge; thus, we must continue to enter new people groups and cities rather than seeking only to consolidate the gains we've made.

9. Will Do Whatever It Takes to Get To The Destination.

- This does not mean that the end justifies every means.

- Rather, it means that we do what our Lord has asked of us, believing that He intends for His church to exist among all peoples before He returns.

- To get to this destination, we must move beyond restrictive thinking, work with world Christian brothers and sisters, and believe He is working in every situation.

10. The Organization Is Not Your God *(Or Your Mother)*.

- Your call is from the One who called Abraham to be a blessing to the nations.

- Your dependency must rest in Him alone. Your power does not lie in the organization's resources or name but in the One who created all things.

- If our worship and allegiance is not focused singularly on the One who made all peoples and, on His Son, then we disqualify ourselves from this race.

Chapter 7
Funding Your Church Plant

It is possible to start a new church successfully with a completely unsupported bi-vocational church planter. It is also possible to raise funds for the new church plant, so the church planters can devote all their time and effort on the church plant. To raise financial support for your church plant you need to communicate the following information to potential donors:

- What are your achievable goals

- How you are stretching to meet those goals

- How the money they are donating will be spent.

- You must also be faithful to keep donors updated about your progress.

Here are some fundraising ideas that were gleaned from several websites:[lvii]

Sending Church Support – Many church plants are funded by the home church that is sending the church planter. This is the best method of support for a new church plant but it is not always possible for the sending church to completely underwrite a new church plant.

Church Planting Networks – There are many church planting networks who partner with local churches to help with the training of church planters and funding the new church plant. Here is a list of a few church planting networks: Association of Related Churches (ARC)[lviii], Acts 29[lix], V3[lx], Soma[lxi], Sojourn[lxii], Church Multiplication Network[lxiii], Stadia[lxiv], and Redeemer City to City[lxv]. In fact, networks are the new normal.

Get others involved - Many church planters receive funding from individuals, relatives, churches other that their sending church and Christian businesspeople. Before approaching individuals, who are involved in local churches, it's a good idea and a move of integrity to get permission from that potential donor's pastor.

Bi-vocational / Tent Making - A secular job can also supply funding for the church planter. If God has called but finances don't follow as expected, the planter can't argue that God has closed the door. Finances are not the determining factor in God's will; God is the determining factor in God's will. Working at bi-vocational employment, at least for a period of time until the church has grown to support the pastor, is a legitimate way to fund a church plant. Having a job gives the church planter a chance to make a connection with the community.

Shared partnership funding model - This model focuses on the plant or planter's funds coming from several sources. First, the church planter should raise funds from friends, relatives, and various churches. Although there are exceptions, if a church planter can't raise funds, the planter probably can't plant a church. Second, the church planter's sending church provides funds. Generally a sending church that does not financially invest in the church plant eventually becomes apathetic toward the church plant and church planter. Third funds come from a church planting network. Being part of one or more of the networks listed above is valuable to a church planter, for these networks would be able to provide assessment, coaching, and training.

Crowdfunding model - Crowdfunding is a method of raising capital through the collective effort of friends, family, customers, and individual investors. This approach taps into the collective efforts of a large pool of individuals—primarily online via social media and crowdfunding platforms—and leverages their networks for greater reach and exposure.

A list of the top 12 Christian Crowdfunding sites can be found at: https://blog.fundly.com/christian-crowdfunding-platforms/

Appendix 1
Church Planting Profile[lxvi]

Introduction

Our goals are to see multitudes of church planters trained and churches planted wherever there is a need including all the remaining unreached people groups of the world. We must be about our Father's work.

The subject matter in this manual has been designed to lay a strong foundation in the church planter's life. It will give him a "war chest" that he can take with him to the battlefield. The key to the planting of churches is the propagation of fivefold ministry. We believe that we have included a series of courses that will not only be foundational in the life of the church planter but serve as mentoring material as he multiplies himself in other church planters.

We will begin this journey with a church planting profile. As you evaluate yourself be honest and open and recognize your strengths and weaknesses. We pray that as you advance through this Church Planters foundations Course you will be strengthened in your weaknesses and made even stronger yet in your areas of strength.

Church Planting Profile

We would like to thank the Evangelical Free Church for their permission to use the written material contained in the Church Planting Profile. The only changes that were made were those to contextualize the material.

This inventory is designed to help you explore your potential as a church planter. In it, we will ask you to compare yourself with effective church planters in four major areas:

☐ **CALL**

☐ **CHARACTER**

☐ **CHEMISTRY**

☐ **COMPETENCIES**

No instrument is 100 percent accurate. People are too complex for that. That is why we use multiple instruments to create a composite picture. This self-assessment is the first step in a comprehensive process to reveal trends and patterns in your church planting profile and determine your potential as a church planter.

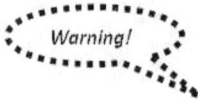

Warning! There are two dangers with self-assessment instruments. First, people do not know themselves. Hopefully by asking a series of reflection questions, this inventory will help you to think deeply about the church planting ministry. Therefore, you need to work through this self-assessment process prayerfully and thoughtfully. Also, you should check the accuracy of your self-assessment with your spouse, pastor, and trusted counselors.

Second, people are not honest with themselves. They are fearful that if they rate themselves too low, it will negatively impact their placement opportunities. Since this inventory is primarily designed to help you discern your own church planting potential, you are free to be completely honest in your reflections.

The reality is that not all pastors are wired to be planters and there is nothing more painful for a pastor than to be ministering in a place where he must constantly operate outside his area of giftedness. On the other hand, there is joy and fruitfulness for the planter who is properly placed in the right ministry environment.

Special Note to Seminarians & Lay Leaders: We believe that recent seminary graduates as well as gifted lay leaders can become effective church planters. Some of this self-assessment is based upon ministry experience. Do not be discouraged by that. That does not mean you cannot be a church planter. It means there are areas you will need to grow in.

Self Assessment Inventory

The Call

It would be foolish for anyone to enter church planting leadership without a clear call from God to do so. Every church planter will encounter obstacles and even opposition to his leadership and will depend upon the certainty of God's calling to carry him through.

Directions:

- Read each reflection statement and then rate yourself from 1 (lowest) to 10 (highest).

- Add up your section total and divide by ten. This is your average rating for this performance dimension.

- Circle your rating for this performance dimension at the top of the sheet and record the rating on the summary score sheet on page 20.

In your opinion, do you have a strong enough call to be an effective church planter?

Call	Clear Sense of God's Call	1	2	3	4	5	6	7	8	9	10

Both husband and wife share a clear and compelling sense of God's calling to be a church planter or founding pastor. That calling is supported and established by fruitfulness in specific areas of ministry and the confirmation of other people in the church.

Clear Sense of God's Call - "In a recent study of failed church plants, half of those leading the failed plant were actually unsure of their call to church planting in the first place! The fact of the matter is church planting can be incredibly difficult. The decision to plant will often be deeply and sometimes painfully tested. Often in the midst of the most difficult times when growth is slow, when leaders you've developed decide to leave, when the next steps forward seem very unclear, the only thing that will keep on going is the sure, unshakable conviction that, 'despite what I'm experiencing now, God has called me to this!' A call is more than thinking church planting is a neat idea, or something you just sort of 'try out' among other options. No, the enormity of such a venture as church planting requires a clarity of calling that, while not immune to doubt, provides the foundation for tenacity during adversity and disappointment."[lxvii]

The Call

Reflection Statements: Rate yourself from one (lowest) to ten (highest) for each question.

_____When I read God's Word, when I pray, when I daydream, I cannot stop thinking about church planting.

_____I am excited about the evangelistic potential of church planting to reach the unchurched.

_____I believe I have a clear call from God to a church planting ministry.

_____Others, such as my pastor and peers, have confirmed my call to a church planting ministry.

_____ My call to church planting has been confirmed by ministry experiences.

_____I believe God has given me the spiritual gifts and temperament to be an effective church planter.

_____I believe many of my life experiences have prepared me to be an effective church planter.

_____In the past, I have taken significant steps of faith that God has blessed.

_____ I have a strong conviction in God's capacity to accomplish great things in a church plant.

_____In spite of the risks, I have a strong inner peace about church planting.

_____**Section Average:** (Total divided by 10)

SELF ASSESSMENT INVENTORY

Character

If a church planter is to be successful, there are two foundational character issues that he must face right at the beginning of his church planting journey. While other skills and qualities are important, these traits are absolutely essential. The Bible is very clear about the importance of character in church planting leadership (1st Timothy 3).

Character:

- Strong Marriage and Spousal Support

- Godly Character

Directions:

- Read each reflection statement and then rate yourself from 1 (lowest) to 10 (highest).

- Add up your section total and divide by ten. This is your average rating for this performance dimension.

- Circle your rating for this performance dimension at the top of the sheet and record the rating on the summary score sheet on page 20.

Character - A	Strong Marriage and Spousal Support	1	2	3	4	5	6	7	8	9	10
	Both husband and wife work together as a team with agreed upon roles in life and ministry. They have a healthy marriage relationship with a well-managed family (1 Tim. 3:4,5).										

Healthy Marriage and Family Relationships - "If married, is the marriage solid and does the spouse support and agree to be involved in the church plant in some way? Without this cooperation, the whole effort comes under a cloud. For something as large and dramatic an undertaking as planting a church, the husband and wife need to be on the same page, in agreement that this is God's calling for them, as well as in agreement regarding the timing of things. To be undertaking something like this and not be in sync with each other is asking for trouble from the very beginning. Better to wait to start the church plant until things are on a more solid footing than to push on ahead and pay the consequences in the marriage and in the church."[lxviii]

Strong Marriage and Spousal Support

Reflection Statements: Rate yourself from one (lowest) to ten (highest) for each question.

_____My wife agrees with and shares my church planting call.

_____My wife knows my church planting vision as well as I do.

_____My wife and I agree upon our respective roles in a new church plant.

_____I am able to balance the demands of ministry and marriage.

_____My wife and I do not have any relationship issues that will negatively impact a new church plant.

_____My wife and I agree upon how we will use our home in a church plant.

_____My wife has no anxieties about our church planting future.

_____My wife and I have strong communication and intimacy so that we are able to share our hearts with one another in all circumstances.

_____My wife and I have no anxieties about raising our children in a church plant at this stage of our lives.

_____My wife and I have regularly scheduled times when we get away by ourselves.

_____**Section Average:** (Total divided by 10)

Godly Character

Character - B	Godly Character	1	2	3	4	5	6	7	8	9	10
The candidate is demonstrating godliness and integrity in his personal, married, and public life. The qualifications for biblical eldership and servant-leadership are evident and he is growing in Christlikeness (1st Timothy 3, Titus 1, Acts 6). His devotional life is a vital factor in his growth.											

Godly Character: While we are not looking for perfect men to give leadership to a church plant, we do expect leaders who are spiritually mature and men of integrity.

Reflection Statements: Rate yourself from one (lowest) to ten (highest) for each question.

_____My devotional life is vital and daily and a major factor in energizing my life and ministry.

_____I maintain a life of sexual purity.

_____I have no unresolved conflicts from my past that have not been dealt with appropriately.

_____I do not have any "skeletons in my closet" which, if revealed, would cause embarrassment to the cause of Christ and my family.

_____My financial house is in order, including the area of indebtedness.

_____I am a good biblical steward of my resources.

_____My ministry associates would say that I have a good reputation in the community.

_____I am teachable in my relationships with colleagues and others.

_____ I have a gentle spirit when I am under pressure or under personal attack from others.

_____When provoked I am able to find resources to keep my anger under control.

_____**Section Average:** (Total divided by 10)

SELF ASSESSMENT INVENTORY

Chemistry: Right Fit

While chemistry is a softer area to assess and sometimes harder to get your arms around, it is critical that a church planting candidate wrestle with the question, "Am I the right fit for this church planting opportunity? Does my personality and leadership style lend itself to church planting? Do I fit the core group and the community in which the church is being planted? Do I fit the model of the church that is being planted?" The following is a list of some of the chemistry areas to be evaluated:

- Doctrinal & Denominational Fit

- Financial Fit

- Core Group & Community Fit

- Church Planting Model Fit

Directions

- Read each reflection question and then rate yourself from 1 (lowest) to 10 (highest).

- Add up your section total and divide by ten. This is your average rating for this performance dimension.

- Circle your rating for this performance dimension at the top of the sheet and record the rating on the summary score sheet on page 133.

Chemistry	**Right Chemistry**	**1**	**2**	**3**	**4**	**5**	**6**	**7**	**8**	**9**	**10**
The candidate "fits" within their Church planting context as determined by his gift-mix, background, and mission of multiplying healthy churches among all the people groups of the world. He also has the ability to minister effectively and live within the core group and community context where he will be placed.											

Denominational Fit: Since we are planting Churches within the context of the church planting movement vision, one of the first things a church planter needs to do is make sure they are in complete agreement with the method and practice of the church planting movement. We are looking for strong leaders, but we do not need lone rangers. We are looking for movement leaders who will take the Great Commandment and the Great Commission seriously and build into the genetic code of their church plant the vision of *"growing healthy churches that multiply and plant other healthy churches."*

Financial Fit: "Church planting does not require you to be a financial genius, but it does require that one knows how to handle money wisely, is out of debt, and has a realistic understanding of the financial needs of a church plant in the beginning years. Debt or irresponsibility with money are prime "plant killers" owing to the pressures and conflicts they bring. Given the financial pressures typically accompanying the first few years of a church plant, a significant amount of debt makes planting very difficult." [lxix] A realistic financial plan needs to be worked out with a church planting coach and Zone Leader.

Core Group and Community Fit: Some church planters have a missionary gift and can effectively minister in any cultural group or community setting. But most church planters have a cultural comfort zone where they minister most effectively. What was the cultural background of your home, high school, and church? What was the size and health of your home church? If there is an existing core group, do your ministry vision and values match theirs? Wise church planters recognize that the larger the community is where they will plant the more varied and identifiable are the lifestyles in that given community.[lxx]

They need to ask God to lead them to a situation that matches their divine design/ministry skill set. The right man in the right place!

Church Planting Model Fit: You fit the requirements of the particular model of church you are planting.

Reflection Questions: Rate yourself from one (lowest) to ten (highest) for each question.

_____I am committed to the church planting movement's Vision.

_____I am committed to the church planting movement mission of *"multiplying healthy churches among all the people groups of the world."*

_____I am willing to be supervised by coaches who are appointed to oversee my labors for Christ.

_____I faithfully tithe my income, live within my means to the glory of God.

_____I do not have financial indebtedness which would prevent me from pursuing church planting.

_____I believe my personality and temperament traits would make me an effective church planter.

_____I believe my spiritual gift mix would make me an effective church planter.

_____My vision and values match the core group that I am going to.

_____My cultural background fits the community setting God is calling me to.

_____I fit the model of the church I am planting.

_____**Section Average:** (Total divided by 10)

SELF ASSESSMENT INVENTORY

Competencies: 10 Skill Sets

The following ten basic skill sets are the kind of skill sets and traits that church planters need to have in order to be effective in their church planting mission. They are based upon a study of scripture (see Ephesians 4 and Matthew 28), a major research project by Dr. Charles Ridley (See *Church Planter's Toolkit*, chapter 2 by Robert Logan), and extensive conversations with Evangelical Free Church planting leaders and other denominational church planting leaders.

Competencies

1. Visionary Leadership Skills
2. Starting-Gathering Skills
3. Communication Skills
4. Evangelistic Skills
5. Discipling Skills
6. Equipping Skills
7. Team Building Skills
8. Group and Leader Multiplication Skills
9. Knowledge of Church Planting
10. Emotional Intelligence (EQ)

Directions

- Read each reflection question and then rate yourself from 1 (lowest) to 10 (highest).

- Add up your section total and divide by ten. This is your average rating for this performance dimension.

- Circle your rating for this performance dimension at the top of the sheet and record the rating on the summary score sheet on page 133.

Competencies - 1	Visionary Leader- ship Skills	1	2	3	4	5	6	7	8	9	10
The candidate has a clear and compelling picture of what the new church will look like in the future and the broad brush strokes of what it will take to get there. He is able to share repeatedly this vision in such a way that others follow his leadership and help make it happen no matter what the cost.											

Visionizing Capacity - "Vision is a God-given ability that is an essential part of the spiritual gift of leadership: an ability to 'see' what could be; in this case, to cast a vision for a church that is compelling and inspires others to want to be a part of it. But a good vision does not just leave it there. Rather, it not only lifts people's sights to what is ahead, but it articulates a way to get there, too. In that light, simply wanting to 'plant a church' is not a 'faith-driven, inspiring vision.' What kind of church? What will it look like? What kind of people will it reach? How will you gather people to get onboard with that vision?

"A church planter must not only have a vision for the kind of church he wants to build, he has to be able to see it, to articulate it in such a way that it engenders faith, and honors God, and inspires other people to want to get on board with the vision, as well.

"Can the person plan out a large, long-term project in a prayerful and yet intentional way? Too many people start off a church plant without a big-picture idea of what it is they are trying to build. They have an idea that they want to try something new, to start a new church, but they lack clarity in their vision beyond the first few steps. Or, even if they are clear in their vision, they lack the abilities to strategically and measurably plan out concrete steps towards accomplishing that vision. The best church planters are those who pray for God's direction ahead of time, plan prayerfully, and then execute the plans."[lxxi]

Reflection Statements: Rate yourself from one (lowest) to ten (highest) for each question.

_____I have a history of starting new ministries, small groups, businesses, etc.

_____I have a clear vision of what God expects my local church to be five years from now.

_____I know the first five things I would do to start a new church plant.

_____I tend to be a "big picture" person rather than a detail person.

_____When I share my vision with other people, they get excited and want to become a part of the team.

_____I have written down the big ideas of my church planting vision.

_____I know what kind of church plant will reach today's unchurched.

_____I can identify the top 5-7 core values of the church I would plant.

_____I have a regular planning process to refine my personal vision.

_____I usually anticipate the "next steps" and see further down the vision road than many of my friends.

_____**Section Average:** (Total divided by 10)

Competencies - 2	Starting-Gathering Skills	1	2	3	4	5	6	7	8	9	10
The candidate has an entrepreneurial, risk-taking spirit and has a history of starting new ministries, groups, or businesses from scratch using only faith, vision, and limited resources. He is able to recruit a diverse group of other people to join with him in accomplishing his vision.											

Starting Skills - Some pastors are good at starting significant things. That ability is demonstrated in their life and ministry experience. Some are good at building on the foundations of others but are unable to be the one who starts things. We will never expect that people in the latter category should be given the assignment of having the first thing they start be a church with all its complexities.

Gathering Skills - "People go about the gathering process in different ways. Some people are good at one-on-one conversations; their gifts and attractiveness naturally come out in personal interactions. Others more naturally gather people with their up-front skills: interacting with large groups, communicating, teaching, and casting vision. 'Gathering people also means being able to attract and empower others who are themselves people-gatherers: people who are extroverts, or who are natural evangelists or "bringers and includers." The leader who is skilled at gathering people will empower those in his core who are natural gatherers themselves because once the church gets to any size at all, his ability to connect with large numbers will be increasingly difficult. The relational connection so necessary to the gathering process in church planting will be more and more dependent on others besides the pastor who are skilled at gathering new people.'"[lxxii]

Reflection Statements: Rate yourself from one (lowest) to ten (highest) for each question.

_____I have started a ministry, business, club, etc. from the ground-floor up.

_____I am able to accept the risks of starting something from scratch.

_____I am able to trust God when resources are limited or scarce.

_____I am able to develop a vision for a ministry that doesn't yet exist.

_____I enjoy working with a wide diversity of people.

_____I am energized by meeting the needs of other people.

_____I do not respond judgmentally toward people whose values and methods differ from mine.

_____I am able to allow others to do the work of people-gathering.

_____I am not intimidated about meeting total strangers.

_____I am able and willing to release people with a confirmed set of different values and ministry philosophy to another church.

_____**Section Average:** (Total divided by 10)

Competencies - 3	Communi-cation Skills	1	2	3	4	5	6	7	8	9	10
The candidate has a proven track record of communicating the Word of God in a relevant and compelling way through his preaching, teaching, and counseling with the result that spiritual fruit and growth are evident. He understands his community context and the unchurched there and is able to communicate to them in their "language" and culture.											

Preaching - "A church planter simply must have good communication skills if the plant is to be at all successful. It does not mean he has to be great. It does not mean he will not improve, probably significantly, and sometimes dramatically, within his first few years of ministry. But it does mean that, as a pastor, he is first and foremost one who preaches the Word. As Scripture unyieldingly recognizes, a pastor must be 'able to teach' (1 Tim. 3:2). There is no getting around the point: church leadership is an inescapably communication-intensive enterprise. What gathers people, what feeds them spiritually, what motivates them to Kingdom-action, what creates a particular church culture is effective communication before large numbers of people."[lxxiii]

Reflection Questions: Rate yourself from one (lowest) to ten (highest) for each question.

_____I place a high value on communicating God's Word and spend a sufficient amount of time to be adequately prepared.

_____I am an effective oral communicator, able to analyze an audience, speak clearly and logically, maintain attention and generate positive response to biblical appeals.

_____I follow a preaching plan that allows me to teach the "whole counsel of God" rather than my favorite passages and themes.

_____I study other communicators to learn how to sharpen my speaking skills.

_____I have the writing ability to communicate my vision in newsletters, brochures, and written articles.

_____I am able to communicate with unchurched persons in my community in a style they can appreciate and accept.

_____I am able to identify and assess the importance of community needs as they relate to the mission of the church.

_____I plan church services and activities with the concerns, comfort, and questions of attending non-believers in mind.

_____My preaching often results in people affirming decisions to trust in Christ and take action concerning God's plan for their lives.

_____I know the first sermon series I would preach in a new church plant.

_____**Section Average:** (Total divided by 10)

Competencies - 4	Evangel-istic Skills	1	2	3	4	5	6	7	8	9	10
The candidate relates well to the unchurched and unsaved and regularly does the work of an evangelist.											

Unchurched - "We must be about building our churches with the unchurched, one way or another, even if we have to go around walls or through windows to do it. If a church is to be healthy, if it is to grow in a biblical way, then the leader should have some sort of evidence of evangelistic orientation."

Barna Study - Interestingly, George Barna did a study contained in his book, *Evangelism That Works* (Gospel Light Books, 1995). Of the churches growing in America due to evangelistic growth, he notes a fascinating (and liberating!) statistic: the majority of the senior pastors of these churches do not have the spiritual gift of evangelism. "But without exception, every single one of them is passionate about evangelism. And that passion carries over into everything they do. It motivates their churches to be evangelistically focused. They consistently find ways to make heroes out of the natural evangelists and gatherers who are in their congregations. And they have worked hard to learn to communicate the gospel in relevant and compelling ways to the unbelievers who are coming to their Sunday services."[lxxiv]

Reflection Questions: Rate yourself from one (lowest) to ten (highest) for each question.

_____I ache over the lostness of those without a personal knowledge of the Savior and pray specifically, and passionately for their salvation.

_____I am proficient in leading people, one-on-one, to a personal knowledge of Jesus Christ as their Savior.

_____I provide regular outreach training events for members of my church to equip them for evangelism and discipling ministries.

_____I enjoy becoming friends with unchurched persons and look for opportunities to do so.

_____Upon moving to a new community, I would spend 50 percent of my time each week in "people contact" work.

_____I urge members and expect leaders of the church I pastor to befriend unchurched people and intentionally seek to attract them to Christ and to our fellowship.

_____I intentionally work to counter the natural tendency of people to become more concerned about their own needs and interests than those of the unchurched.

_____I am committed to the concept that we must work evangelistically to reach people of other cultural backgrounds whether they live nearby or in other parts of the world.

_____I am willing to forego programs and conveniences that are standard in my colleagues' churches if they are not appropriate to my community setting.

_____I know the evangelistic events I would plan in the first year of the church plant.

_____**Section Average:** (Total divided by 10)

Competencies – 5	Discipling Skills	1	2	3	4	5	6	7	8	9	10
The candidate has the ability to help develop Christian maturity in individual believers and build up the body of Christ by creating relational environments that nurture spiritual growth.											

Two Challenges - There are two challenges at this point. One is to help the believer move away from consumer Christianity to Biblical discipleship where a life is marked by obedience (John 14:15) and service (Mark 10:45).

The second challenge is to help the new believer to grow and to begin to take ownership of ministries in the church plant.

Teaching - The primary skill the planter uses in building both individuals and church bodies is the teaching of God's Word. This teaching must not be just cognitive. It must be oriented toward life transformation (2nd Tim. 3:16-17). The purpose of teaching is not knowledge, but life obedience (Mt. 28:20). The planter needs to help individuals develop spiritual disciplines in their lives. The planter needs to understand process training and the importance of sequencing. The planter needs to develop an intentional disciple making process that can move people from one level of spiritual maturity to the next level of maturity (e.g. Class 101, Class 201, Class 301).

Reflection Questions: Rate yourself from one (lowest) to ten (highest) for each question.

_____I am actively discipling new believers.

_____I am actively involved in a small group.

_____I understand the spiritual maturation process and know how to move people to the next step of maturity.

_____I make personal goals for spiritual growth each year.

_____I have a good grasp of Scripture and know where to point people for practical help with their problems.

_____I am familiar with the best discipleship training materials for spiritual growth.

_____I have a strong gift of teaching.

_____I have helped new people own the vision of the church.

_____I consistently help established group members discover ways to involve newcomers in the church.

_____I know the orientation class I would develop for welcoming new people to a church plant. I am committed to a constant process of multiplying discipleship leaders so that the capacity for disciple making will increase.

_____**Section Average:** (Total divided by 10)

Competencies - 6	Equipping Skills	1	2	3	4	5	6	7	8	9	10
The candidate demonstrates the ability to help others discover, develop, and use their spiritual gifts in suitable ministries.											

Equipping - The church planter must quickly move from the role of being the primary player to being a player-coach. His primary orientation is not doing but discipling and delegating. This sounds like an incredibly easy change to make. But the reality is that it is exceedingly difficult to pull off. That is why the vast majority of churches in America are under 100 people in size.

Gift Based Ministry - The key in this role change is that people see the planter as one who is helping them develop their spiritual gifts and their individual potential, rather than becoming his "helpers" to fulfill his ministry goals. This means the planter must be receptive to the leading and gifting of our Sovereign Lord. He must build ministries and programs that are gift based, rather than tradition driven. The planter must design a ministry that helps believers discover, develop, and then deploy their giftedness. Spiritual gifts training can be de-motivating if there is not an outlet for expressing this giftedness in ministry.

Reflection Questions: Rate yourself from one (lowest) to ten (highest) for each question.

_____I believe it is my job to equip the laity for works of ministry, and I do this diligently.

_____I regularly seek to match other church members' spiritual gifts with ministry needs.

_____I do not try to meet all the ministry needs myself.

_____I recognize my own limitations and gladly delegate responsibilities and authority to others.

_____I provide adequate training for others before assigning them to specific ministry tasks.

_____Others do not feel they must always have my permission before initiating new ministries.

_____I give high priority in my ministry time to equipping others.

_____I am able to spark interest in the appropriate ministry goals of our church and help people respond to achieve those goals.

_____I carefully monitor group morale and avoid placing unrealistic expectations on members.

_____I can develop orderly structures to maximize the effectiveness of a local church's ministries and resources.

_____**Section Average:** (Total divided by 10)

Competencies - 7	Team-Building Skills	1	2	3	4	5	6	7	8	9	10
The candidate is a servant-leader who can identify, recruit, and build a team of people made up of others who complement his gift-mix and role preference, and who follow his vision for ministry.											

Lay Leadership Development - "In a church planting study of failed church plants, the number one characteristic associated with an unsuccessful church planter was this: They were unable to identify, recruit, train, and deploy lay leaders. It was an overwhelmingly prominent statistic that 95 percent of unsuccessful church planters faltered in this category.

The undeniable truth is it takes a person with a certain mix of gifts and catalytic abilities to pull off planting a church. Among the most important is that they must be able to attract and lead other leaders! They need not only internal spiritual authority, but also basic, pragmatic competence in growing a church if they are to attract, motivate, and train others around them who can also lead. If a church planter can lead people to Christ and nurture them but cannot develop and lead leaders, he will not be able to build much more than a large home group. The church will never grow beyond what the church planter himself can directly oversee and lead."[lxxv]

Reflection Questions: Rate yourself from one (lowest) to ten (highest) for each question.

_____I am constantly looking for new, young leaders to disciple.

_____I can recruit other leaders who share a sense of responsibility for the growth of our church.

_____I know the kind of leaders I need to complement my own spiritual gift mix.

_____I have discipled leaders to the point where they have taken over ministry.

_____It is easy for me to delegate ministry to other qualified leaders.

_____I have designed a training program for equipping lay leaders.

_____I am not threatened when lay leaders excel at ministry skills beyond my own.

_____I know the first staff position I would want to fill.

_____I see my primary role as helping other leaders succeed in their ministries.

_____I read leadership books and attend leadership seminars to sharpen my leadership skills.

_____**Section Average:** (Total divided by 10)

Competencies - 8	Group and Leader Multiplica- tion Skills	1	2	3	4	5	6	7	8	9	10
The candidate has the ability to unite diverse people in groups that accomplish a common vision, and which multiply. He is able to multiply leaders and groups so that more can be accomplished. As a result of his multiplying skills, he can lead a new church to grow beyond the 100 and 200 barriers.											

Multiplication - The planter has a track record of multiplication. He is constantly thinking multiplication. He is not just thinking addition. He is not just thinking, "How can I get people in the front door and assimilated in the church?"

He is thinking reproduction. He is thinking, "How can I move people around all the bases and create grand slam disciples?" He is thinking, "How can I multiply this church with new daughter churches?"

In a growing church plant, the planter quickly discovers he must multiply ministry options.

Reflection Questions: Rate yourself from one (lowest) to ten (highest) for each question.

_____I know what it takes to build positive morale in a church body.

_____I know how to handle "difficult people" so that they do not destroy group morale.

_____I have a track record of multiplying believers and disciples.

_____I have developed leaders who have, subsequently, developed a new generation of leaders.

_____I have led a small group to the place where it multiplied into two groups.

_____Groups that I have led have multiplied past the second generation. (That is, the first group produced a second group and the second produced a third.)

_____I have trained leaders of different sized groups (small, mid-sized, and large) and have utilized them in multiplying such groups.

_____I have trained leaders for groups with a variety of purposes and used them to multiply groups and ministries.

_____I understand how my pastoral role will have to change as the group grows. I know how to lead a church plant through the 100-200 growth barriers.

_____**Section Average:** (Total divided by 10)

Competencies - 9	**Knowledge of Church Planting**	1	2	3	4	5	6	7	8	9	10
The candidate possesses and applies a growing knowledge of church planting, church health, and church growth. He demonstrates an observable and practical commitment to the vision of "growing healthy churches that multiply and plant healthy churches."												

Pastors of dying and plateaued churches often complain about church growth as only being "market driven, business stuff." Pastors of growing, healthy churches are pastors who continually develop their knowledge of church planting, church health, and church growth.

Effective church planters want to know what is working and what is not working. They want to know why some churches are growing and why some churches are not. They want to understand church health in order that their church might grow and reproduce. This is not idle curiosity for them, nor is it an ego trip. Church planters count lost people because lost people count. Effective church planters understand that people may reject their message. Effective church planters, however, do not want the message rejected based on outdated methodology. Therefore, they are committed to constantly develop their knowledge base of effective church planting, church health, and church growth.

Reflection Questions: Rate yourself from one (lowest) to ten (highest) for each question.

_____I am committed to establishing spiritual, as well as numerical growth goals.

_____I believe a church plant should be fully self-supporting financially within 36 months of launching its first public worship service.

_____I am uncomfortable in the role of a "maintenance" minister, one who is expected simply to keep an organization functioning smoothly for the satisfaction of its present members.

_____I view responding to the Great Commission as the top priority of my church.

_____I see non-growth of the church as a threat to the future of God's work in my community.

_____I have read at least three resources on church planting. They are

_____,

_____, and

_____.

_____I am committed to planting a daughter church within three-five years of our first public worship service.

_____I have taken special classes or attended workshops on church growth and church health.

_____I can identify three major church growth principles I would immediately apply to my church plant

_____I have church planting eyes. I am always looking for new places to start new churches.

_____**Section Average:** (Total divided by 10)

Competencies - 10	Emotional Intelligence	1	2	3	4	5	6	7	8	9	10
The candidate can easily adjust to the challenging and rapidly changing environment of a growing new church. He is flexible and adaptable and has demonstrated the ability to persevere and bounce back quickly from even the most difficult circumstances while pressing on because of a Spirit-guided inner call or motivation.												

Flexibility and Adaptability - Church planting can be both tremensdously exciting and horribly discouraging and lonely. A church planter needs to have the emotional maturity to ride the highs and lows of the emotional roller coaster of church planting. On the one hand, the first rule of church planting is being flexible and adaptable. Murphy's law was invented and perfected to an art form in a church plant. A healthy church planter must have the ability to laugh at himself. A church planter should not take himself too seriously. A person with a rigid personality will not be happy in church planting.

Resilience and Tenacity - On the other hand, a church planter must have the tenacity and persistence to stick it out when the going gets tough. There will be times when your vision will be tested, when leaders quit on you, and when neighboring pastors will oppose you. Resilience is one of the traits of an effective church planter. Church planting is not for the faint-hearted.

Intrinsic Motivation: Self-Starter - A church planter does not punch a clock. In the beginning stages, there is little structure in church planting. A church planter often works without direct supervision. Therefore, it is critical that a planter know how to manage his time and manage himself.

Reflection Questions: Rate yourself from one (lowest) to ten (highest) for each question.

_____I am flexible and can easily adjust to changes found in the early days of church planting.

_____I am resilient and can stick with a task despite the discouragements inherent to church planting.

_____I can bounce back quickly in times of disappointment and when others hurt me.

_____I am a self-starter and can work at difficult tasks without supervision.

_____I am good at managing my time and completing assignments.

_____I manage my emotional life without being hijacked by it.

_____I can read other people's emotions without being told.

_____I can skillfully handle the feelings of others in ministry relationships.

_____I can articulate the unspoken pulse of a group I am ministering to.

_____I have a growing understanding of who I am in Christ.

_____**Section Average:** (Total divided by 10)

Self-Assessment Summary Score Sheet

Name: _____

Address/City/Zip: _____

E-mail address: _____

Telephone (   ) _____

Current ministry position: _____

Church/Denominational Affiliation:_____

Record the scores from your self-assessment worksheets below:

Call	Low	Medium					High		
Clear Sense of God's Call	1 2 3	4 5 6	7	8	9	10			
Character	Low	Medium					High		
A. Spousal Support	1 2 3	4 5 6	7 8 9 10						
B. Godly Character	1 2 3	4 5 6	7 8 9 10						
Chemistry	Low	Medium					High		
Right Fit	1 2 3	4 5 6	7 8 9 10						
Competencies: 10 Skill Sets	Low	Medium					High		
01. Visionary Leadership Skills	1 2 3	4 5 6	7 8 9 10						
02. Starting-Gathering Skills	1 2 3	4 5 6	7 8 9 10						
03. Communication	1 2 3	4 5 6	7 8 9 10						

Skills										
04. Evangelistic Skills	1	2	3	4	5	6	7	8	9	10
05. Discipling Skills	1	2	3	4	5	6	7	8	9	10
06. Equipping Skills	1	2	3	4	5	6	7	8	9	10
07. Team Building Skills	1	2	3	4	5	6	7	8	9	10
08. Multiplying Skills	1	2	3	4	5	6	7	8	9	10
09. Knowledge of Church Planting	1	2	3	4	5	6	7	8	9	10
10. Emotional Intelligence (EQ)	1	2	3	4	5	6	7	8	9	10

In your opinion, do you have strong enough traits and skills to be an effective church planter? It is important that you check out your self-assessment with your spouse, pastor, and closest friends to get an accurate assessment.

Bibliography

Borthwick, Paul, *How to Be A World-Class Christian*, Wheaton, IL, Victor Books, 1993

Clark, Jim, *101 Things Every Pastor Should Know*, Xulon Press, 2004

Depew, Michael, *Paul and the Contextualization of the Gospel*, www.pages.preferred.com/~mdepwe/mis1.html

Donovan, Vincent J., *Christianity Rediscovered*, New York, NY, Orbis Books, 1983

Eckhard, John, *Leadershift: Transitioning from the Pastoral to the Apostolic*, Chicago, IL, Crusaders, 2000

EFCA Start Church Planters Boot Camp Manual,

Fuller, W. Harold, *Mission Church Dynamics,* Pasadena, CA, William Carey Library, 1980

Frost, Michael, *Translating the Gospel*, www.cegm.org.au/-resources/translating%20the%20gospel.htm

Gallagher, Neil, *Don't Go Overseas Until You've Read This Book*, Minneapolis, MN, Bethany Fellowship, Inc, 1977

Garrison, David, *Church Planting Movements: How God Is Redeeming A Lost World*, Midlothian, VA 2004

Gaukroger, Stephen, *Your Mission, Should You Accept It... An Introduction for World Christians*, Downers Grove, IL, Intervarsity Press, 1996

Georges, Jason, *The 3-D Gospel: Ministry in Guilt, Shame, and Fear Cultures*, Time Press 2016

Goll, James W, *Lost Art of Intercession,* Destiny Image 2007

Havlik, John F., *Evangelizing and Congregationalizing*, Atlanta, GA, Home Mission Board, S.B.C., 1977

Hesselgrave, David J., Rommen, Edward, *Contextualization: Meanings, Methods, and Models*, Pasadena, CA, William Carey Library, 2000

Hesselgrave, David J., *Planting Churches Cross-Culturally A Guide for Home and Foreign Missions*, Grand Rapids, MI, Baker Book House, 1980

Hiebert, Paul G., *Anthropological Insights For Missionaries*, Grand Rapids, MI, Baker Book House, 1985

Hiebert, Paul G., *Anthropological Reflections on Missiological Issues*, Grand Rapids, MI, Baker Book House, 1994

Hogue, C. B., *I Want My Church to Grow*, Nashville, TN, Broadman Press, 1977

Hodges, Melvin L., *The Indigenous Church*, Springfield, MO, Gospel Publishing House, 1953

International Bulletin of Missionary Research, Vol. 39, No. 1, also World Christian Database, 2015, *Barrett and Johnson. 2001. World Christian Trends.

Jenkins, Philip, *The Next Christendom: The Coming of Global Christianity*, New York, NY, Oxford University Press, 2002

Johnson, Todd, *Global Atlas of Christianity.*

Krallmann, Gunter, *Mentoring for Missions*, Waynesboro, GA, Gabriel Publishing, 2002

Lingenfelter, Sherwood, *Agents of Transformation*, Grand Rapids, MI, Baker Books, 1996

Little, Paul E., *How to Give Away Your Faith*, Downers Grove, IL. InterVarsity, 1966

Marchant, Don, *Equipped to Go To An Unreached People*, Ramona, CA, Vision Publishing, 2004

McGavran, Donald, *Understanding Church Growth*, Grand Rapids, MI, William B. Eerdmans Publishing Company, 1970

Monthly Missiological Reflection #17 May 2001Downloaded from http://www.missiology.org/mmr/mmr17.htm,

Moore, Ralph, *Starting a New Church: The Church Planters Guide to Success*,

Nicholson, Steve and Bailey, Jeff, *Cutting Edge Magazine, Winter 1998*

Peterson, Roger and Gordon Aeschliman and R. Wayne Sneed, *Maximum Impact Short-Term Mission*, Minneapolis, MN, STEM Press, 2003

Reimer, Albert M., *Comparison and Evaluation of a Church Planting Project (Mother Church Concept)*, Deerfield, IL, Trinity Evangelical Divinity School, 1982

Richardson, Don, *Eternity in Their Hearts*, Ventura, CA, Regal Books, 1984

Samuel, Vinay and Chris Sugden, *Mission as Transformation*, Carlisle, CA, Regnum Books International, 1999

Schaeffer, Francis, *Escape from Reason*, Downers Grove, IL, Inter-Varsity Press, 1968

Tiplady, Richard, *One World of Many? The Impact of Globalization on Missions*, Pasadena, CA, William Carey Library, 2003

Van Rheenen, Gailyn, *Missions: Biblical Foundations & Contemporary Strategies*, Zondervan, Grand Rapids

Warren, Rick, *The Purpose-Driven Church*, Grand Rapids, MI, Zondervan, 1995

Web Evangelism Guide web-evangelism.com, used with permission – http://quide.gospelcom.net/resourses/strategy.php

Zachary, Rick, The Master of Relationships: How Jesus Formed His Team, Baker, LA Keepsafe, 2004

Notes

[i] Marchant, Don, <u>Equipped to Go to the Unreached People</u>, Vision Publishing, Ramona, CA, page 30

[ii] http://www.thetravelingteam.org/stats

[iii] International Bulletin of Missionary Research, Vol. 39, No. 1, also World Christian Database, 2015,*Barrett and Johnson. 2001. World Christian Trends, pg 656

[iv] International Bulletin of Missionary Research, Vol. 39, No. 1, also World Christian Database, 2015,*Barrett and Johnson. 2001. World Christian Trends, pg 656

[v] International Bulletin of Missionary Research, Vol. 39, No. 1, also World Christian Database, 2015,*Barrett and Johnson. 2001. World Christian Trends, pg 656

[vi] Todd Johnson, Global Atlas of Christianity, pg 296,

[vii] International Bulletin of Missionary Research, Vol. 39, No. 1, also World Christian Database, 2015, *Barrett and Johnson. 2001. World Christian Trends, pg 656

[viii] Todd Johnson, Global Atlas of Christianity, pg 296,

[ix] Baxter, Mark R. 2007. The Coming Revolution: Because Status Quo Missions Won't Finish the Job, pg 12.

[x] *The New King James Version*. (1982). (Ps 96:7–10). Nashville: Thomas Nelson.

[xi] Gallagher, Neil, Don't Go Overseas Until You've Read This Book, Bethany Fellowship, Inc, Minneapolis, MN, 1977 p. 94

[xii] Gaukroger, Stephen, Your Mission, Should You Accept It... An Introduction for World Christians, Intervarsity Press, Downers Grove, Illinois, 1996 pp 17, 19

[xiii] © Web Evangelism Guide web-evangelism.com, used with permission – http://quide.gospelcom.net/resourses/strategy.php

[xiv] Ibid., Web Evangelism Guide

[xv] Op. cit., Marchant, page 227,228

[xvi] Ibid., Marchant, page 229

[xvii] Ibid., Marchant, page 231

[xviii] Ibid., Marchant, page 231

[xix] Ibid., Marchant, page 231

[xx] Ibid., Marchant, page 233-5

[xxi] Ibid., Marchant, page 231

[xxii] Ibid., Marchant, page 236

[xxiii] Hesselgrave, David J. and Edward Rommen, Contexualizaion: Meanings, Mehtods and Models, Pasadena, CA , William Carey Library

[xxiv] Hodges, Melvin L., The Indigenous Church, Gospel Publishing House, 434 W. Pacific St., Springfield, MO 1953 p. 2

[xxv] Donovan, Vincent J., Christianity Rediscovered, Orbis Books, Maryknoll, New York, Third Printing, November 1983 p. vi

[xxvi] Donovan, Vincent J., Christianity Rediscovered, Orbis Books, Maryknoll, New York, Third Printing, November 1983 p. 30

[xxvii] Op. cit., Marchant, page 32.

[xxviii] Downloaded from http://www.missiology.org/mmr/mmr17.htm, Monthly Missiological Reflection #17 May 2001

[xxix] Ibid., Monthly Missiological Reflection #17

[xxx] Ibid., Monthly Missiological Reflection #17

[xxxi] Downloaded from http://guide.gospelcom.net/resources/context.php article titled "Contextualization"

[xxxii] The 3-D Gospel: Ministry in Guilt, Shame, and Fear Cultures, by Jason Georges, Time Press 2016, page 56

[xxxiii] Ibid, page 10-11

[xxxiv] Frost, Michael, Translating the Gospel, www.cegm.org.au/resources/-translating%20the%20gospel.htm

[xxxv] Ibid., Frost

[xxxvi] Ibid., Frost

[xxxvii] Ibid., Frost

[xxxviii] Depew, Michael, <u>Paul and the Contextualization of the Gospel</u>, www.pages.preferred.com/~mdepwe/mis1.html

[xxxix] Ibid., Depew

[xl] Little, Paul E., <u>How to Give Away Your Faith,</u> (Downers Grove, IL: InterVarsity, 1966). p 83.

[xli] https://nazarene.org/article/mission-briefing-redemptive-analogies

[xlii] https://www.gatewaycwm.org/sites/gatewaycwm.org/files/Team%20 training%204.2%20Redemptive%20Analogy.pdf

[xliii] Van Rheenen, Gailyn, <u>Missions: Biblical Foundations & Contemporary Strategies,</u> Zondervan, Grand Rapids, p.

[xliv] Ibid., Van Rheenen

[xlv] https://www.peterdehaan.com/spiritually-speaking/micro-church/

[xlvi] https://www.brainyquote.com/quotes/quotes/h/henryford121997.html

[xlvii] James W. Goll, *Lost Art of Intercession*, p. 28

[xlviii] James W. Goll, *Lost Art of Intercession*, pgs. 23-25

[xlix] James W. Goll, *Lost Art of Intercession*, p.16

[l] Ralph Moore, *Starting a New Church: The Church Planters Guide to Success* , p.65

[li] *EFCA Start Church Planting Boot Camp Manual*, p.14

[lii] Moore, p.237

[liii] Moore, pgs. 117-120

[liv] Moore, p.126

[lv] *Bootcamp*, p. 24

[lvi] Moore, p.187

[lvii] The ideas for this chapter came from article from the following websites: https://get.tithe.ly/blog/church-plant-fundraising; https://www.churchplanting.com/funding-new-church-plants/#.XyeyISgzY-U; https://newchurches.com/blogs/church-planting-and-funding-facilities/; https://influencemagazine.com/Practice/How-to-Finance-Your-Church-Plant; https://www.fundable.com/learn/resources/guides/crowdfunding/what-is-crowdfunding

[lviii] https://www.arcchurches.com/

[lix] https://www.acts29.com/

[lx] http://thev3movement.org/

[lxi] https://wearesoma.com/

[lxii] https://www.sojournnetwork.com/church-planting

[lxiii] https://churchmultiplication.net/

[lxiv] https://stadiachurchplanting.org/

[lxv] https://redeemercitytocity.com/

[lxvi] We would like to thank the Evangelical Free Church for their permission to use the written material contained in the Church Planting Profile. The only changes that were made were those to contextualize the material.

[lxvii] *Cutting Edge Magazine, Winter 1998, Steve Nicholson and Jeff Bailey*

[lxviii] *Ibid.*

[lxix] *Ibid.*

[lxx] *See Percept Demographics*

[lxxi] *Ibid.*

[lxxii] *Ibid.*

[lxxiii] *Ibid.*

[lxxiv] *Ibid.*

[lxxv] *Ibid.*

www.ingramcontent.com/pod-product-compliance
Lightning Source LLC
La Vergne TN
LVHW021506080426
835509LV00018B/2418